Martial Arts

Martial Arts

Peter Lewis

Published by Magna Books
Magna Road
Wigston
Leicester, LE8 2XH

Produced by Bison Books Ltd.
176 Old Brompton Road
London, SW5 0BA
England

ISBN 0 948509 60 0

Printed in Hong Kong

Reprinted 1988

Page 1: *Master Y C Chang executing a posture from the tai chi form. Note how the back leg supports his full body weight as he moves forward into the next stance.*
Page 2: *A ninja performing a cartwheel maneuver.*

Page 4-5: *Silhouetted against a background of the setting sun, two martial artist's battle it out on a mountain top. Duels between samurai could last from two minutes to several hours, but fights are now forbidden.*

CONTENTS

INTRODUCTION

The original concept of the martial arts incorporated a total system of training that went far beyond fighting. The arts were intended to take practitioners past the violent antagonism of hand-to-hand combat to a radical transformation of their very being. The martial arts established a unique trinity of fighting, philosophy and religion from which their devotees cannot escape. For the essence of the martial arts is that they are not just concerned with conquering an opponent, but with coming to terms with oneself and the universe. In other words, fighting has been transported from an animal instinct into an exact science informed by eastern religious doctrines. These doctrines have been taught for thousands of years by great sages and philosophers who have found that, by channelling your energies through the martial arts, mind, body and spirit are united, and it is possible to become one with nature and the universe. The martial artist works towards the same goal as that pursued by Indian yoga practitioners, but takes a different route. Instead of channelling mental and spiritual energy into meditation, he or she takes a path paved with great hardship and demanding physical effort. In time, and through total dedication to the task at hand, a very different person begins to emerge. A person freed of self-doubts and inadequacy. Pessimistic failures can be transformed into optimistic successes. Yet the martial arts also enable the student or adept to achieve a passive mental state while remaining capable, at all times, of springing into action with a deadly array of fighting skills to tackle any situation.

Along this 'great way' of learning, the devotee transcends physical combat to enter the realms of philosophy in searching out the meaning of life. The disciple seeks to comprehend what the Chinese term 'the three great ultimates' – man, earth, and heaven – discovering how they are connected within the order of the universe.

This search for inner peace might seem an unlikely goal for those joining a kung fu or karate club, intending to master self-defense, but it is the essence of the traditional martial arts. They are a series of stepping stones that lead the adept away from the pitfalls and self-regard of the ego to a wiser, more generous personality, benefiting both the martial artist and society.

The martial arts can be many things to many people. For some they are the perfect vehicle for achieving physical fitness, while others regard them as an ideal means of self-protection in a violent age. But they can also be much more than that, and can lead to a path of self-discovery and self-renewal. It is completely up to you how far you travel and how much you achieve.

A hand-tinted photograph of Japanese samurai, and a perfect example of the traditional weapons and costume of the era.

Above: *The Shaolin Temple, Hunan, China. It is said that all martial arts originated here.*
Above left: *A rubbing from a tenth century carving of Confucius and one of his disciples by Wu*
Tao-tzu from the Confucius Temple at Peilin.
Left: *A Taoist tapestry from the Ming Dynasty. The symbols represent magical incantations connected with alchemy.*

religion of Taoism (pronounced Dow-ism) followed the concept of yielding or non-action. Its aim is to achieve a peaceful mind without the extremes of either anger or happiness, a mind without worry. Through these ideas and the exercises which are their material expression, a good, healthy and long life can be achieved (longevity has been a constant source of inspiration to the Chinese). Taoism proposes that all things in the universe exist perfectly in a state of harmony; the concept of uniting apparent opposites in a constant flow is the essence of the religion.

Buddhism arrived in China from India, where various divisions then took place. Eventually different sects were established, some became barely recognizable from the original source in India. One sect that was to have a profound effect upon the martial arts was Zen. Zen, or Cha'n as it was known in China, was established at a monastery high in the Songshan Mountains at Shaolin, the birthplace of *kung fu* according to legend.

Followers of Zen Buddhism believe that the center of meditation and the seat of mental power is a point on the body situated about two inches below the navel called the *tantien* or *tanden*. The significance of Zen is that it provides the underlying philosophy within the martial arts. A beginner in martial arts enters the place of training full of his own opinions and thoughts. The novice must empty the mind to become a vehicle for new learning, to drink in knowledge, to become open-minded.

Zen has an aid for emptying the mind ready for meditation, the *koan*. A *koan* is an illogical and unanswerable question upon which the student must concentrate, which automatically empties his or her mind of day-to-day trivia. A typical example of a *koan* is the question, 'In clapping both hands a sound is heard; what is the sound of one hand?' The answer is not within the field of ordinary human reasoning. The individual continues to solve the problem, concentrating upon nothing else. Suddenly, the answer, or perhaps more correctly, *an* answer, becomes apparent. Even if the answer is not decipherable, the Zen student does not give up, for his life is his will, and his will is his Zen faith. A knowledge of these principles of

Above: *A young Chinese factory worker demonstrating a tai chi form with double swords. Tai chi sword is the most advanced stage of the art. Children train in martial arts from as early as nine years old as an aid to health and fitness. Once the form is learned, the students progress to the weapons of the kung fu system they are learning.*

Zen gives an understanding of the mentality of the Japanese samurai, and how they looked upon death as having little meaning. One cannot know the martial arts simply by reading about them, they have to be experienced at a personal level before understanding is gained.

In historical terms Taoism and Buddhism went hand in hand, the Chinese never really separating the two religions to any great extent.

However, for the moment we are mainly concerned with Taoism, which is the life force of all the Chinese martial arts. To the Chinese, everything in life has its opposite, which unites in harmony to become the cosmos. A symbol of these two opposing forces flowing into one another in a continuous state of change are the *yin* and *yang*, the positive and negative aspect of the universe. Neither can exist without the other. These two inseparable forces (seen in the symbol of a black fish with a white eye, and a white fish with a black eye on a circular diagram) represent the true roots of all Taoist philosophy. Just as the two complementary forces flow into one another so season follows season, night becomes day, hard becomes soft, the yin becomes the yang and then becomes the yin again. These two apparent opposites are not permanent and irreconcilable but constantly change in a ceaseless rhythmic cycle. Understanding this interchange of yin and yang is perhaps the single most important aspect in learning a kung fu system. Chinese martial arts are all based on either the nature of soft or hard, action and non-action, which is why Taoism and its philosophy played such an important role in their development.

Both Buddhism and Taoism shared similar approaches to medicine, believing that the mind and body should not be viewed as distinct enties, but are inseparable. Taoists believed that certain breathing exercises would aid them in their search for longevity. The regulation of breath became a preoccupation with the Taoists and it became a strict religious exercise and established the basis for the internal system of Chinese boxing *nei chia chuan*.

This breathing system cultivates what the Chinese refer to as *chi* (vital air). They believed that although chi was an intrinsic force inherent in all human beings it had to be cultivated through the Taoist breathing exercises. The vital chi force was further complemented by the action of the *i* (mind), which directs the energy throughout the body. The ancient Chinese called this principle mind force, the harnessing mechanism or agent for mental powers and physical prowess. Chi energy is utilized in the Taoist-inspired art of *tai chi chuan* (great or grand ultimate fist); the mobilization of the inner strength of mind produces more strength than can be exerted by sheer muscle power alone.

Borrowing some Buddhist doctrines, the Taoists created two great books, which contain sets of deep-breathing exercises, philosophical ideas and diet programs. The two volumes are the *I-chin Ching* (muscle change) and the *Pa Tuan Chin* (eight-section brocade). These two books were the basis of the internal system of Chinese boxing. The history of Chinese medicine records the close ties between the Taoist search for immortality and the development of the martial arts. Chinese medicine, religion, and martial arts developed through interacting with each other.

The Chinese martial arts developed at three levels: the Buddhist-influenced Shaolin Temple, the Taoist-influenced Wu Tang (Wah Lum) monastery, and the village arts of the peasants themselves. According to legend an Indian prince, the son of a Brahman king in southern India, renounced all his riches and titles and adopted the mantle of a wandering monk. His aim was to master the Buddhist doctrine of *Mahayana* which involved searching into one's own being to discover freedom and enlightenment. Meditation (known in India as *dhyana*) was an essential ingredient of this search. Originally dhyana used meditation to control the mind and focus its force upon one point; this concentrated focus is similar to the martial arts principle of transfixing one's physical strength and energy upon a single vulnerable point on the opponent's body. This *Ch'an* meditation, as it was termed in China, aimed at stripping the mind of all feelings and passions. The monk changed his name to Bodhidharma, (Ta-Mo in Chinese) and began his long quest in search of enlightenment. It is said that he sat with his face to a wall for nine years, meditating while listening to the ants screaming. After reaching enlightenment Bodhidharma travelled to China to preach his doctrine, as he was saddened at the decline of the orthodox teachings of Buddha in China.

After wandering through much of southern China he ventured to the north and travelled through the wild mountainous regions, finally arriving in the province of Honan (Hunan). He sought refuge at the temple of Shaolin, which was partly derelict but was still occupied by a few monks. The monastery had been built 150 years previously in honor of the Buddhist master Bhadra but during the Chou dynasty Buddhism was prohibited by order of Emperor Wu, and the monastery forced to close. It reopened 50 years later, and had since been run with a skeleton staff who taught the Buddhist *sutras* to anyone who would listen.

Left: *An early painting of Bodhidharma, the wandering Buddhist monk who established a series of health-giving exercises among the monks of the Shaolin Temple. From these exercises developed what is known as Chinese boxing or kung fu.*

Right: *A group of tai chi chuan practitioners outside the Temple of Heaven in Peking, going through the tai chi short form. The movements are slow, with great emphasis on posture and balance. Practitioners concentrate on breathing and fluidity of form. During the exercise all outside thoughts are swept away and only the task at hand is deemed important. It is for this reason that in the West tai chi is highly regarded for relieving stress and tension.*

Below right: *A solitary practitioner going through the movements of the tai chi form. He is completely oblivious to his surroundings and concentrates only upon getting each posture correct. Millions of Chinese practice this solo form every day.*

Bodhidharma entered the monastery to find that the years had taken their toll on both the structure and the resident monks. Their failing health was all too apparent, and Bodhidharma quickly initiated a series of health-giving exercises based on the deep breathing techniques of yoga. The monks' haggard features and physical debilitation soon became a thing of the past. This special system of breathing and exercising became known as the 18 Hands of Lo-Han (Lo-Han means a disciple of Buddha). These exercises formed the basis of a formalized system of temple boxing, which later evolved into a complete fighting system for self-defense.

Input from other types of kung fu, usually gleaned from wandering priests seeking refuge or boxing masters from other styles seeking out Shaolin for further knowledge, led to the establishment of the martial tradition of Shaolin. For over a thousand years the monastery flourished and distinct fighting styles emerged, each with its own subtleties. Disciples were taken into the temple confines as apprentices, providing that they could pass certain tests. These tests were based on loyalty, honesty, endurance, dedication and psychological makeup. Prospective students, all male children under the age of 10 years (women were not accepted for training until the latter

part of the sixteenth century), were brought by their parents or guardians to the temple walls and left outside to await acceptance. To test their endurance the abbot would sometimes leave the budding disciples waiting for days on end, but he secretly kept a close watch to see how they behaved. The children waited patiently and silently to see what transpired. In time, some of the children would play child-hood games. These were the failures and would never see beyond the high walls of Shaolin. The remainder were given a series of menial tasks to test them yet further. They had to learn to tolerate the hardships of servitude for at least three years. During this period the young novices were pushed beyond the limits of normal human endurance. Each day they carried two large cast-iron buckets to the bottom of the mountain to fill them up with water from the stream; they had to make the arduous trek back up the mountain with full buckets without spilling a drop. In the second year the young disciples had to wear solid iron shoes weighing over 20 pounds on their daily trek down the mountain. As the months passed many budding monks fell by the wayside, unable to keep up with the hard tasks and returned to their homes. The few that were finally left were deemed fit to carry on the tradition of Shaolin, and were ordained as priests. The disciples did not realize that the three years of hard training, carrying the water up and down the mountain, was really aimed at making their bodies fit and strong enough to undergo the strict martial arts training they would receive once ordained.

When the disciple became a priest his head was shaved bald and his skull was scorched nine times with lighted incense, creating nine scars. Only then could he be termed a Shaolin monk and a proper kung fu training schedule could begin. The monks swore a secret oath never to divulge any of the techniques they were taught. The martial training was based on the fighting patterns of five animals: the dragon which represented spirit; the snake for toughening the bones and tendons; the tiger for strength; the leopard for breath and the crane for stamina.

Many kung fu styles are based on careful observation of animals fighting. An animal, having no rational mind, moves freely and impulsively in attack and in defense. When studying a system based upon one or more particular animals, the aim is to become like that animal, learning through training to imitate the nature of the beast. A kind of metamorphosis takes place, both mentally and physically, whereby the student identifies with the animal and it becomes an extension of his own body. If unexpectedly attacked an adept can quickly offer a defense by employing the strength of a tiger, or perhaps evade the initial confrontation and then counterattack by adopting a pose from the monkey style. The student's defensive actions are executed sharply and unconsciously, by pure reflex action, imitating the monkey's agility by leaping, jumping, and rolling.

Kung fu was developed not only for self-defense but also as an invaluable health-giving exercise. Training in one of the many kung fu styles consists of learning and practicing prearranged movements, called sets or forms, choreographed by the ancient masters to simulate countless combatative situations. These movements constitute a series of toughening-up exercises combining speed and reflex training.

The Shaolin monks spent many years at the temple learning not only kung fu but also medicine, including herbalism and acupuncture. Philosophy and translating the Buddhist sutras into Chinese was also part of their daily program. Eventually the novice monk/priest was ready to leave. Tradition dictated that he would have to undergo one final test before going out into the world, known as the 'wooden dummies' lane. The 'wooden dummies' were in fact skilled practitioners of Shaolin kung fu. About 30 of them would hide inside the long corridor that led to the main gate. The would-be challenger walked in complete darkness down the corridor and was ambushed at intermitent stages by the hidden masters. They attacked him with kicks and punches, palm strikes and finger jabs. The recipient would have to evade them all and retaliate effectively. Very often the departing monk would not even make it halfway before he was stopped by an eye-gouging technique from the tiger-claw system, or struck down with a paralyzing finger strike from a dragon stylist. Only the very best made it to the end of the lane.

Those who succeeded were met at the end of the corridor by a huge bronze stove or cauldron which held burning incense. This barred their path to the outside door. To leave the temple the monk would have to move the great pot. On the sides of this cauldron were carved a dragon and a tiger (some historians claim it was decorated with two dragons). The monk, in a type of bear-hug lift, pressing his forearms against the red-hot walls of the stove, pushed the great pot to the side. In executing this frightening task the monk's forearms

Right: *The tai chi practitioner executes the form in a slow, relaxed manner so that each posture blends with the next. There is no age limit in tai chi, young and old alike practice the art. Its prime purpose is to promote health and longevity. The pose this practitioner is about to enter into is the single whip.*

received the imprint of the dragon and tiger. These permanent tattoo-like burns were his 'graduation certificate,' informing the world that he was a master of Shaolin kung fu. The front gate of the temple was only ever opened to allow a fully trained fighting priest passage to the outside world. Other than this, all entrances and exits at Shaolin were made through a side door.

Much has been said and written about the original Shaolin Temple (known as Sil Lum in Cantonese), debating whether or not it really existed at all. What appears to be the original temple was built in AD 495 by royal decree of the great emperor Hsiao-Wen. It was predominantly Buddhist in faith, and was probably the forerunner of later such temples throughout China. It has often been argued that the wide range of martial arts in China could not all have originated at the legendary Shaolin. Many could have started in Taoist temples, which are also known to have housed fighting monks. The main Taoist temple was called Wah-Lum.

In AD 698 Emperor T'ai Tsung of the T'ang dynasty called upon the fighting monks of Shaolin to aid him in his war against General Wang-Shih-Ch'ung, who had gathered a large army in an attempt to oust the T'ang emperor from the Imperial throne. According to legend 13 monks answered their emperor's plea although in fact it was a much larger force. The emperor's army, with the help of the Shaolin monks, was victorious and the enemy was routed. In recognition of their great action T'ai Tsung awarded the monks land, and bestowed upon the temple the title, 'Number One

Above: *Part of a national wu shu troupe exercising in the tai chi form. In China practitioners often train near water because the water encourages a state of calm and tranquility.*

Monastery Under Heaven.' For the next thousand years Shaolin prospered and more and more Chinese turned to Buddhism.

In 1647, during the Ching dynasty, an event occurred that was to have repercussions that would still be felt up to the twentieth century. As if history was repeating itself, a decree was sent from the emperor in Peking to Shaolin appealing to the monks for assistance in defeating the invading hordes attacking China's eastern borders. Once again the fighting monks gathered together an army and joined the emperor K'ang-Hsi and his troops in the conflict. The warlord bandits were defeated

and the monks resumed their vocations in Shaolin. However, court officials convinced the emperor that he should disband the force of fighting monks, as they could prove to be a threat to the throne because of their amazing fighting capabilities. At first the emperor did not listen, but constant plotting persuaded the emperor to issue orders that the temple at Shaolin should be destroyed and the monks dispersed.

Aided by a renegade Shaolin monk, who showed the emperor's forces a secret passageway into the grounds of the temple, the imperial army sacked Shaolin and razed it to the ground. Overwhelmed by a surprise attack and sheer force of numbers the monks were put to the sword; only 128 survived. These 128 were constantly persecuted and two years later only five were left alive. They managed to cross the Yellow River to eventual safety. These survivors, known as the 'Five Ancestors,' were called Hung, Monk, Lau, Li, and Choy. They pledged to set up their own monasteries as centers of resistance against the Ching dynasty (this supports the theory of there being more than one Shaolin monastery).

The five ancestors are credited with establishing the first *triad* secret society. The word triad comes from a Chinese symbol representing heaven, earth and man. The triads were closely involved in two of the greatest revolts of the nineteenth century: the Taiping uprising against the Manchu rulers and the famous Boxer Rebellion of 1900. This last rebellion was fought against the spread of Western influence, and was led by the chief of the I-Ho-Chuan (Society of Righteous and Harmonious Fists), Ts'ao fu-T'ien. The term 'boxers' was applied by the British because of the many kung fu fighters taking part in the revolt. After the overthrow of the Manchus and the establishment of a republic in 1911, the triads gradually lost much of their power on the Chinese mainland and fled to Hong Kong and Chinese settlements overseas, such as New York and San Francisco, where they became involved with criminal activities such as drug trafficking and protection rackets. Even today all triad recruits are trained in the unarmed combat skills of kung fu. For years the police forces of Western countries refused to believe such a mafia-like organization existed and information regarding the triads is only now coming to light. Their activities are well illustrated in the movie *The Year Of The Dragon.*

Since China's cultural revolution, relics of the past have been rebuilt and the Shaolin Temple in Hunan has been fully restored and is preserved as a historic monument. Because of the popularity of Chinese martial arts in the West, Shaolin has become a major tourist attraction.

Chinese kung fu is generally divided into two broad approaches. The nei chia chuan fa (internal fists school) stresses the metaphysical and philosophical aspects of kung fu, and comprises three styles, tai chi chuan, *pa kua*, and *hsing i*. These 'soft styles' use the concept of yielding to an attack rather than meeting it head on, epitomizing the Taoist principle of non-action. They neutralize an opponent's attack without exerting unnecessary energy.

The second approach is *wei chia chuan* (external styles fists). The external or hard systems are associated with power strikes and hand and body conditioning. They utilize force in a straight line with a certain emphasis on kicking techniques. The external systems are generally associated with Shaolin and Buddhism, whereas the internal systems are directly linked with Taoism.

The internal styles concentrate on the will, vital energy (chi), to develop inner strength. The Taoist techniques of deep breathing (*chi kung*) cultivate the chi energy in the body and the martial art practiced makes use of that energy. Internal or soft systems are considered to be defensive, while the hundreds of external boxing styles are usually more aggressive and muscular in approach. The soft styles devote greater attention to the maintenance of balance and concentrate on smaller, subtle and effective circular movments. The most popular internal style practiced today is tai chi chuan.

Tai chi, as it is more commonly referred to, is a type of moving meditation. This art emphasizes complete relaxation and suppleness, an expanded, open awareness which includes rather than concentrates, and a mental emotional attitude of calm, detachment and harmony. The movements are flowing and continuous. No direct resistance is offered when the tai chi exponent is attacked. The aggressor, finding no place for his attack to land, is swept around and tossed to the side like a leaf in the wind. The tai chi exponent uses a series of throws and pushing motions; these merge with the attacker's momentum to guide him spirally to the ground, defeated.

Tai chi chuan has been described as the

Above: *The practitioner slips from an open-palm strike to a full-fist punch. His internal energy will transmit the power through the strike into an opponent's body. Once struck, an opponent would experience great internal disturbance, which often results in death.*

Top: *A tai chi student enters into a long stance,* indicating the combat side of the art. His open palm is indicative of a strike to a vital organ.

Above right: *Combat practitioners must return to the peacefulness of the form. So after any practice using combat tai chi, all students go through the full tai chi exercise to bring back a state of non-hostile and tranquil thought.*

ultimate martial way of life: it is an exercise for health, a martial art, and a pathway to philosophical wisdom. Its creation is attributed to the Taoist philosopher Chang San-Feng. Legend relates that during the Yuan dynasty (1206-1333) Feng retired to the mountains to seek solitude and experiment in alchemy, searching for the secret of immortality. After making and drinking a strange herbal concoction, he fell into a deep sleep, during which he had a strange dream. The voice of heaven cried out to him and guided him through a series of fighting maneuvers using the tactic of always yielding to attack.

Upon awakening he wrote down the movements he had been shown in his dream and began to practice them everyday. In less than two years his bent frame began to straighten up and he regained vigor and vitality. His whole body took on a youthful appearance. Feng thought he had finally found the elixir of life.

During his travels he was attacked many times by roving bandit gangs, whom Feng quickly dispatched to their ancestors using his new-found tai chi skills. His fame spread far and wide, prompting an admirer of his fighting system, Chen Chia Kou, to ask Feng if he could become his disciple. The master took him under his wing and over the following ten years taught the young adept everything he knew about tai chi chuan. Upon his master's death (folk tales relate that Feng lived to be 200 years old) Chen Chia Kou returned to his home in northern China. He had promised to keep the art a secret, even to any member of his own family whose character was questionable. For the next 400 years the Chen family kept tai chi a secret by only practicing at midnight.

The most popular style practiced in the West today is *yang tai chi*, developed by Yang Lu-Shan. Yang was a great Chinese boxer, well versed in the martial arts of his homeland. He had heard of the great chen-style boxing and of the family's almost pathological urge for secrecy. In an attempt to learn tai chi, Yang Lu-Shan became a servant in the Chen household, but could not find their place of practice or see the family training.

Then, late one night, Yang heard muffled noises. Upon investigating he found the family training in a slow, hypnotic kind of swaying dance, and knew he had found what he was looking for. Unknown to the family Yang spied on the practice sessions month after month, diligently practicing what he observed. Eventually he was caught spying by the head of the Chen family, Chang-hsing, who was so angry that he set his students on Yang. But Yang had learned his lessons well, and defeated them all. Chen's anger turned to delight when he saw that Yang was a gifted boxer. Chen departed from tradition by taking Yang on as his closest student.

Chen felt his style had strayed away from the original guiding principles and before his death, asked his disciple to reform the system and make slight changes. Yang moved to Peking and began to make the modifications his master had asked. When he had perfected the system Yang Lu-Shan became one of the greatest boxers in the Imperial City. His fame spread to the emperor, who asked Yang to teach his personal imperial guard the techniques of his newly named Yang-style tai chi. Regarded as one of the best fighters in the city, Yang became a target for jealous rivals who fancied themselves as equally great boxers. One famous story relates that Yang was attacked by five thugs envious of his popularity. They knocked him to the ground, where he just curled up into a ball while they beat him. The next day Yang walked into the town apparently unhurt and not a mark on him. His attackers had all been rushed to the local infirmary suffering from severe internal injuries.

Yang's grandson Cheng-fu was probably the greatest tai chi fighter ever. He was able to knock a person out with a single light push of his hands, his contemporaries said that Cheng-fu yielded with the softness of cotton, and his push penetrated like a bullet. Today the Yang style tai chi chuan is the most popular style practiced in the West. In the parks and waterfronts of San Francisco Chinese masters can be seen each morning teaching their students, young and old alike, the principles of this ancient exercise.

In essence, tai chi chuan is the Taoist practice of bringing positive and negative forces into harmony, uniting the body and its surroundings through a formalized exercise called the 'form.' Over the last hundred years tai chi styles have splintered into four main groups: *chen, yang, wu,* and *sun.* During the cultural revolution in China all the great tai chi masters were gathered together. They formulated a tai chi exercise called the 'short form' consisting of just 24 steps. It comprises all the various movements from the other forms but is condensed into a quick and easy method for learning tai chi. The main elements of tai chi are retained without all the repetitions found in the other forms. This 'modern version' was established to make the Chinese healthier and cut down on the number of working days lost through illness. The execution of the short form takes less than five minutes to perform and yet retains all the health benefits of the longer versions.

The movements of tai chi are designed to allow the body to move in a relaxed, smooth and fluid manner. Today the combat side of the art is looked upon as secondary. Because tai chi is very calming and soothing, it has become very popular in the West for the relief of stress. New York, for example, boasts lunchtime classes in tai chi, which can reduce stress by practicing for as little as an hour a day.

Left: *Sifu Y C Chang performs a movement from the tai chi form known as step back and repulse the monkey.*

Below left: *Master Pan Wing Chow (left), a Chen-style tai chi master, exhibits the two-man exercise known as pushing hands with a student.*
Below: *Master Liao executes his tai chi form in a darkened room. When practicing the form surroundings matter little, which is why it is often referred to as moving meditation. One could go through the form in a busy street and be oblivious to the activity all around.*

Right: *Tai chi master Sifu Lam prepares to demonstrate the amazing power of his chi energy. Standing in the classic horse stance, five people bear down on him using all their strength. Applying his chi energy outwards, Sifu Lam repulses all his would-be attackers (below).*
Far right: *Tai chi practitioner Daniel Connor typifies the calm and tranquil tai chi exponent as he trains in the tai chi short form.*

The combat side of tai chi embodies the principle of non-resistance, or yielding. By yielding the practitioner redirects the attack. Tai chi does not use blocks and strikes as do many other martial arts. If we use the circle as a description, tai chi takes the movement around the circle and back into the aggressor with great force. But it is not muscular force, it is internal energy which bests the opponent. Even though tai chi is practiced very slowly and the 108 movements of the solo exercise seem mesmeric in appearance, they are very dynamic in their structure. And even though not apparent when performing the solo form, the internal energy emitted is very powerful indeed.

During training basic principles are emphasized and should be strictly adhered to to gain maximum health and combat benefits. They are: complete relaxation through slow and correct postures; rigidity and strength must be emptied from the upper torso and sunk to the lower abdomen region, with the feet firmly planted on the ground; and relaxed breathing must be maintained by using the diaphragm instead of the upper chest muscles. Only in the flexibility of the waist is there any true strength, because the waist is the foundation of all bodily movements. It is the ability of the practitioner to use the waist, to co-ordinate the whole body behind the movement, that gives strength.

In tai chi the body is always upright, the body skeleton hangs as though suspended from the crown of the head, relaxed through all joints so that the weight of the body sinks downward and the practitioner eventually falls into a natural and relaxed posture. Tai chi begins in 'stillness,' it is the physical embodiment of the principle of non-doing, non-acting. The movement originates and is generated from this stillness. From not-doing, from letting go, comes the stillness that ultimately creates the motion. The energy produced and used in tai chi is likened to an iron bar wrapped in cotton wool. On the outside it is soft and gentle, but within, it has the hardness, power and energy of, as the old Chinese saying goes, 'ten thousand men.'

The second of the internal kung fu systems is *pa kua* (eight trigrams) and, like tai chi, is based upon the *I-Ching*. The I-Ching (Book of Changes) is one of the oldest books in the world, dating back more than three thousand years. This great book is still used by the Chinese as a method of divination. It is an oracle which 'contains all the knowledge of the world,' and is also a manual of philosophical and moral doctrines. The *I-Ching* and the *Tao Te Ching* (The Way and the Power) are the two essential works on Taoism. The *I-Ching* concerns the eight trigrams which formalize the interplay of the yin and yang. These trigrams are further combined into 64 hexagrams which form the 64 chapters in the Book of Changes. The hexagrams purportedly relate to all things under heaven and in nature. The practice of pa kua is supposed to be the middle link between tai chi and hsing-i.

The yin-yang symbol is always seen surrounded by the pa kua or eight trigrams. The sequence in which they are arranged dates back to antiquity and was tremendously important not only in the internal martial arts but also in traditional Chinese medicine. The sequence begins with *ch'ien*, which was the creative principle and regarded as heaven. It is represented as three straight yang lines. Its direct opposite is *k'un*, or earth, which is represented by three broken lines. K'un is the passive principle. The permutations between three straight and three broken lines are 64. The

eight trigrams, whose arrangement is attributed to King Wen, are known as the sequence of later heaven.

Pa kua is based upon the principle that if a fighter can defend himself at all eight points of the compass he will be fully protected from an attack from any direction. The practice of pa kua movements correspond with the eight trigrams, placing great emphasis on turning in a circle throughout the whole duration of an attack. The art has very few linear maneuvers. All students of the art begin by learning an exercise to gain competence in pa kua's unique stepping patterns, known as 'walking the circle.' As in tai chi, pa kua has one central form which is the foundation from which the rest stem. This is called the 'Great Mother Form' or *da mu hsing*. The aim of the practitioner is to develop the ability to move around an opponent, circling him constantly in an attempt to find an opening in his adversary's defense in which to strike.

Basically pa kua has eight steps and eight palm/fist strikes which can be permutated into 64 different techniques. While walking the circle the student must bend his legs until the heel, buttocks, and knees form a triangle, with the weight of the body evenly balanced on both legs. This builds up power in the legs and abdominal muscles. Rather than actually punching an opponent, the practitioner uses palm strikes with the open hand. The four basic strikes are the vibrating palm, crushing palm, lightening palm, and overturning palm. An understanding of the footwork and the palm strikes, along with the spiralling and twisting body maneuvers, enables the practitioner to evade an attack and circle behind his opponent, to strike at the rear or from the side. In appearance, a pa kua student looks as if he is walking in one direction and looking in another direction, while hitting or striking in a third direction.

Since pa kua is a nei chia system there is a special emphasis on developing the *chi gung* (internal power). Chi is a difficult concept for the Westerner, who usually associates strength with huge frames and rippling muscles. Chi rules the three internal systems above all else; even many external kung fu styles incorporate chi development, though not to the epic proportions as the nei chia systems. Chi can perhaps best be explained by an example. The press reported a car crash involving a woman and a child. The child was trapped beneath the wrecked car, and the 128-pound woman, in a frenzy of fear and concern, lifted the front end of the car to free the child. This seemingly impossible feat of strength actually happened. The woman, under great stress, blocked out her rational mind and performed a feat her conscious mind would not have even considered. In effect it was intrinsic energy, chi, acting in an uncontrolled situation. Likewise lunatics are said to have the strength of ten men.

Imagine applying chi to a fighting discipline and spending a great number of years perfecting the technique of controlling it. The

power inherent within that individual is phenomenal, as has been known to the Chinese for over 3000 years. Acupuncture is based on treating the chi centers in the body, which are termed meridians. Because of this link, it is not uncommon for kung fu masters to be accomplished doctors of traditional Chinese medicine.

But developing chi energy is perhaps the hardest quality to master in the art. During training a pa kua student learns the single-palm change and the double-palm change. Every action is circular, which includes the torso's ability to revolve and rotate. Though relaxed at all times the practitioner's body is likened to a coiled spring. Pa kua experts do not attack directly but move behind an opponent and upset the balance and harmony of the antagonist. The waist is the body's major axis and leads every action. Deep breathing is maintained at all times. Paradoxically, pa kua is defensive and evasive in attack. The central theme of pa kua is one of change; the circling movements totally confuse the opponent. Blending in with an opponent's attack rather than directly contending it is the absolute priority. Because there is no fixed stance in pa kua, there is little point in standing rooted in

Left: *An exponent of pak mei kung fu delivers a palm-heel strike to an attacker's chin, competently blocking the incoming fist-strike. This technique is used in conjunction with an open-palm strike, known as a willow-leaf palm, to the opponent's sternum or abdomen. The elongated stance of the defender allows him to place his leading leg forward, between his attacker's legs, thus preventing the latter from instituting a kick because his first line of attack has failed.*

Right: *A pa kua master correcting a student's technique. Relaxed movements are essential for proper application; stiffness or rigidity would impair the effectiveness of the technique.*

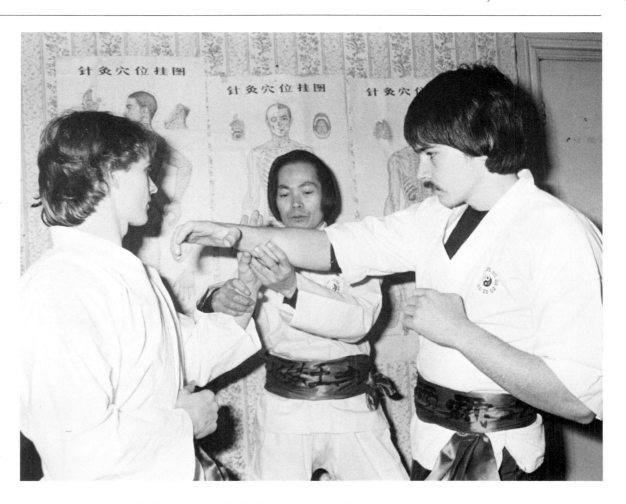

one position. Fixed stances reduce mobility and maneuverability. Therefore every movement and posture in the art is transitional. Training drills in pa kua are practiced solo.

According to legend the pa kua symbols were arranged in order by the sage emperor Fu Hsi in 2852 BC. Hsi arranged the solid and broken lines of the pa kua which represent the polarities of yin and yang after studying the markings etched into the shell of a sacred turtle which appeared one day on the banks of the Yellow River.

Pa kua chang, as it is more commonly known, first came to the attention of martial artists a little over 200 years ago. Its purported founder, Tung Hai-Chuan, was a eunuch who worked at the Imperial Palace of the Ching emperor, Tao Kuang. His early life was spent in and around Hopei province, where he had to be constantly one step ahead of the authorities because of various misdemeanors. Eventually Tung fled his village and went to the mountains to lie low for a time. He entered a monastery to improve his limited boxing skills, but the abbot expelled him less than a year later because of his habitual drunkenness and general misbehavior. He headed deeper into the mountains, destined to become a bandit.

While foraging for food one day, he came across an old Taoist hermit performing a strange dance-like routine. The hermit's body was twisting and spiralling up and down; he walked backward and forward in a circle, changing his direction every few seconds. Although Tung thought he looked about 80 years old, the hermit was moving with the agility of a 20-year-old. Marking the old man as an easy target to rob Tung rushed in and attacked him. He was instantly enmeshed inside what he thought was a hurricane. He spiralled into the air and crashed to the ground more than 20 feet away. Three times he attacked, and each time he was thrown like a rag doll to the ground. Regretting the error of his ways, Tung approached the hermit for instruction. Agreeing to Tung's plea, the old man taught him pa kua. Tung spent more than 10 years in the mountains before coming back to civilization.

We next hear of Tung when he is in the service of the emperor. During a great festival a banquet was held at the royal court. Guests had been invited from all over the kingdom and the palace was thronging with people. Tung, who was acting as a waiter, was slipping in and out of the guests, carrying trays of drinks without spilling a drop. He twisted and turned around

in all directions, weaving in and out. This was brought to the attention of the emperor, who could not believe that a servant could work so fast without spilling a drop of wine. When asked how this was possible Tung answered that it was due to his training in kung fu. Immediately he was challenged to fight by two white crane masters employed by the emperor. Tung accepted the challenge and soundly beat both of them with very little trouble.

After this Tung became famous as a very capable fighter throughout Peking. He was never beaten, except when he fought Kuo Yuen-Shen practicing the hsing-i chuan system. After the bout both men made a binding pact that all of their future students would be instructed in both internal styles, so none would ever come into direct contention with one another. To this day this pact has never been broken. Tung only ever taught 22 students the complete system because it was so time consuming to learn.

The last art of the internal trinity is hsing-i, which is the hardest of the internal systems (in application rather than in degree of difficulty). Unlike pa kua, the movements in hsing-i are based largely upon linear movements linked with solid footholds. All hsing-i strikes occur

directly on a line with one's nose, and are mostly centered upon the opponent's nose. Thus the nose serves as a guide for all attacks. In a hsing-i strike, the weight is reversed, so that the front leg receives the greater proportion of one's own weight. The art stresses the use of vertical strength and fists; and works upon the geometric principle that the shortest distance between two objects is a straight line. This straight-line theory is emphasized throughout training, and students are instructed never to retreat but always to advance head on.

Hsing-i means mind and body; the practitioner aims at uniting his mind with his body before committing an attack. Since it is an internal art the power of the punch comes from within the body, no tension is applied to the fist at all. The energy erupts at the point of impact, and has the force of an 80-pound sledge hammer. However, the physical techniques of hsing-i are secondary to mental development. As in the other internal arts, hsing-i stresses the development of chi.

Hsing-i reflects the Chinese belief that the yin and yang work through the five elements of wood, fire, earth, water, and metal. Each element has the power to overcome the other. Wood conquers earth, earth conquers water,

Above far left: *An attack is initiated, but is instantly blocked with a rising backfist.*
Above left: *Stepping in quickly, the defender now becomes the attacker and converts his block into a ridge-hand strike to the throat.*

Above: *Still using the same hand, the defender now puts his body weight behind the strike, while delivering a kick to his attacker's kneecap.*
Above right: *The attacker falls under the kick, and is finished off with a forearm strike to the base of the skull.*

water conquers fire, fire conquers metal, and metal conquers wood. This tennet symbolizes the primeval law of heaven and earth. Each of the five postures in hsing-i is associated with one of these elements. Furthermore, the five elements are directly related to certain internal organs of the body. Metal is related to the lungs, wood to the liver, water to the kidneys, fire to the heart, and earth to the spleen. Practicing hsing-i strengthens these organs, thus promoting constant good health.

In solo training the mind of the hsing-i boxer is free from imaginary opponents and fighting tactics. Instead, he trains to develop a calm mind that embraces and controls every action of his body. The major form in hsing-i is the five-element form. Mastering it takes a great deal of time and training. In this form, the elements are represented through the five basic movements, which are identified as splitting, crushing, pounding, drilling and crossing. This framework contains the primary movements to cover all angles and directions of attack and defense. As in other styles, the basic movements have thousands of variations, but they are all executed at a very high speed.

When a student has mastered the foundation of the five elements he goes on to learn the form which links the separately practiced movements into a pattern of connected sequences. This is called *lien hwan chuan*. Like many other schools of Chinese boxing, the traditional methods of hsing-i adopt a series of postures imitating the mannerisms of animals. Some instructors concentrate on all 12 animals, while others teach only a few. Although students learn all these forms, technical competence is usually demonstrated in only two or three of them.

Over a period of years hsing-i evolved into three distinctive schools. These were: the traditional style under Kuo Yuen-Shen; a natural school under Wang Hsiang-Chai; and a modified version developed by the famous Sun Lu-Tang, who died in 1933. The traditional and

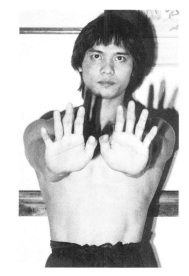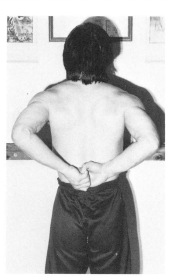

most popular method of training today is the five-element form method. This utilizes stances similar to other systems of kung fu, and stresses techniques based on very definite patterns. For example, the practitioner executes a series of quick, sharp blocking and striking techniques while moving forward in an alternating left/right action. His foot patterns are executed both lineally and obliquely. From this training, a hsing-i stylist learns the role that each part of his body plays in the delivery of force. The shifting of weight, co-ordination of hands and feet, negative and positive must all be understood before one can transmit true power.

Hsing-i was possibly the brainchild of the twelfth-century Chinese general, Yueh Fei, who was also the accredited author of the famous Chinese classic on health exercise, *Pa Tuan Chin*, written during the Sung dynasty.

During the K'ang-hsi period (1662-1772) two schools are known to have been practicing hsing-i, the Shansi school under Tsao Chi-Wu, and the Hunan school under Ma Hsueh-Li. But following the death of the head of the Shansi school, hsing-i training moved to Hopei province and divided into three branches from which all present-day hsing-i has evolved.

Chi kung, another 'soft' form, is essentially a health exercise which promotes long life through a healthy body. Its history can be traced back over 2000 years. Recent archaeological finds in a tomb at Changsa, in northern China included a silk painting from the Han dynasty, (206 BC to AD 220) which depicts diagrams of 30 chi kung breathing postures. The great Chinese classic the *Nei chia*, the Yellow Emperor's treatise on internal medicine, again over 2000 years old, stresses the cultivation of the 'vital air,' if one is to remain healthy and achieve longevity.

To the martial arts practitioner, the proper cultivation of chi provides new heights of mental and physical awareness, increased stamina, and sharpened perceptions. The harmonization of chi is the goal to which all martial artists aspire. Through the special breathing techniques and subtle body movements the flow of chi energy is increased within the body.

Because chi cannot be seen, but only felt and experienced, doubt has been cast in the West as to its existence. However, the great success of acupuncture and acupressure in treating both chronic conditions and acute diseases in recent years has persuaded many medical practitioners that this vital, invisible force really does exist.

An area of kung fu that specializes in chi kung training for a specific purpose is the 'Iron Palm.' Students begin by being treated with *dit dow jar*, a special herbal liniment made to a secret recipe. This liquid is regularly massaged into the hands and arms to make the skin thick and impenetrable. Coupled with complicated breathing methods, this quickly develops chi. After six months or so the student is given punching bags filled with rice, and six months later the rice is replaced with iron sand. The time spent punching the bags lengthens from perhaps 10 minutes every other hour to 30 minutes every hour.

Once iron-palm training has begun the student has to maintain a strict, healthy lifestyle. The student must sleep for the correct amount of time and train at the exact time every day. If a practice is missed or even delayed, the student must start again from the beginning.

Above left: *This series of pictures shows basic chi kung breathing techniques. Left to right: Sifu Austin Goh increases the vital air flow around his body by breathing in with his fists clenched. He then expels the air as he crosses both palms over his chest. In the next exercise he pushes outwards with his open palms, exhaling. Clenching his fists behind his back, he then breathes in. The final exercise uses a clenched-palm grip with the elbows raised while breathing in.*

Above: *Sifu David Lea stands calmly as darts are hurled into his back. By utilizing his chi energy he feels no pain whatsoever.*

The old masters used to say that training for iron palm is like a man paddling a canoe against the current. If he stops paddling, even though just for an instant, the canoe does not stop too, it slips back with the current. During a period of anything up to five years the student trains on bags, punches in thin air, alternately hits a bucket of wet sand and a bucket of water, thus bringing out the hard and soft principles of the yin and yang.

By the time training is over, the adept will be able to summon chi at will, and channel it to any area of the body required. The iron-palm practitioner can kill an opponent simply by touching them on a specific area of the body. So sophisticated is this talent that the user can even predict the exact time the recipient will meet his death following the moment he touched the unfortunate victim. This ability is known as *dim mak* (death touch). Just the slightest touch can cause massive internal damage to the vital organs without marking the victim's body using the time strike. It was rumored in Hong Kong that Bruce Lee's death was caused by a time strike from an iron-palm master he had offended. However, there is absolutely no evidence to support this supposition at all, as shall become clear in the following chapter.

Nowadays iron-palm gung (taken from the chi kung) is used to cure the sick and ailing. This is facilitated by the master moving his chi energy to his fingertips and transfering it to the patient's body. Countless patients undergoing this treatment have reported a slight vibrating sensation. In effect, the chi kung master is actually unblocking the chi energy channels of the sick people. Their recovery rate is quite phenomenal.

In kung fu demonstrations the master will often impress a gathered crowd of spectators by smashing his fingertips or open palm through slabs of concrete and roofing tiles without damaging his limbs. One wonders how is this possible, without the aid of some unseen super power?

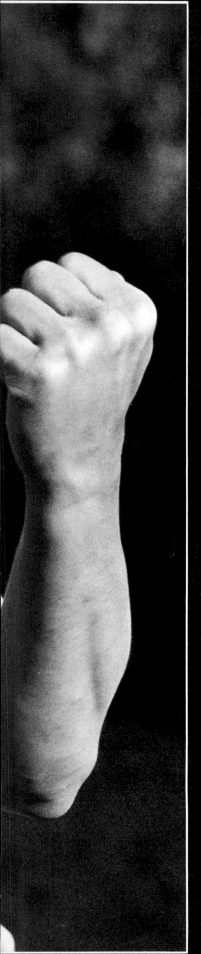

THE EXTERNAL KUNG FU SYSTEMS

A reflection on a pool of water does not reveal its depth

A typical pose from a
kung fu system called
Shaolin Fists. This style is
a hard/soft style. It
originated in Shaolin
Temple in ancient times.

To understand kung fu it is essential to become familiar with the underlying philosophies, principles and themes which inform all the Chinese martial arts. The fighting styles of the multitude of systems have been adapted from the animal kingdom, the insect world and even from the heavenly constellations.

The study and practice of kung fu in China was carried out in schools that were tightly bound together like a family unit. The head of the kung fu family is the *sifu* (teacher). The sifu was like a father figure, and the advanced students, sihings, were looked upon as older brothers. The place of training is called a *kwoon*, where all practitioners of a kung fu school worked under a system based on self-discipline and sacrifice. It is because of this dedication that the Chinese martial arts as we know them today have survived.

The earliest recorded fighting style is the primitive *chih yu hsi* style, dating from the Chou dynasty (1122-255 BC), which proves beyond doubt that a systematized combat form existed in China long before Bodhidharma's visit. The legendary Huang Ti is said to have used chih yu hsi to defeat the chihyu monster, after which many varied forms of kung fu sprang up in villages all over China. Some were developed still further, with refinements being added by different masters over the centuries. Some of today's styles have borrowed their names from earlier systems. Others have used techniques from a particular type of kung fu as a central core and elaborated on the system. Hung gar (hung kuen) developed in this way; although this style depended upon five animals for its working techniques just the tiger and crane were used to create a new fighting concept.

This selective approach creates a hybrid kung fu system. In some cases the new style is a great improvement on the original, but in the early days, when kung fu was beginning to flourish, this borrowing and modifying led to diluted and inferior styles. Some excellent kung fu styles completely died out when a master did not have a senior student to whom he could pass on his technique. Because of the Chinese obsession with secrecy, a master would not commit anything to writing. Today, much of the kung fu seen in the People's Republic is gymnastic, rather than a functional self-defense combat form.

Generally speaking kung fu can be divided

Left: *A Chinese rebel of the early 1900s. These soldiers of warlords were termed 'boxers' by the Western occupiers of Peking, because their kung fu skills were thought to resemble Western boxing.*

into either internal or external categories. In the previous chapter we saw the development of the internal systems into the twentieth century. There are only three main types of internal kung fu, but at a conservative estimate there are in the region of three thousand distinct

Left: *Miss Chen Tao-yun posing with the long-tassel sword, or rainbow sword. A traditional Chinese wu shu item, it is often seen in displays and demonstrations. The swords are usually made from aluminum, and are consequently very light and easy to handle.*

types of external kung fu. It is usually accepted that *wei chia* (external arts) are divided into two broad types, the northern *Sil-Lum* and southern *Sil-Lum*, with the Yangtze River being the demarcation line between the two. The northern styles of kung fu tend to have very long and graceful movements, and display a large number of high kicking techniques. In the south the techniques are short but very powerful, requiring a certain amount of muscular strength in their execution. The footwork of these southern styles contains solid movements in short steps, with very few kicks above the waist.

In English the term kung fu is a general one, but the exact meaning is somewhat ambiguous, meaning a task, work performed, special skills, strength and ability, time spent, and exercise.

With the demise of the Manchu government in 1911 and the birth of the People's Republic the following year, Chinese boxing spread further across the land. Warlords and bandit chieftains devastated China and boxers from the many schools of kung fu allied themselves to these political figures. By 1928 *wu shu* (war arts) were renamed *kuo shu* (national arts) and a formal boxing-training program was established on a national scale. Different styles emerged, especially from the mid-Chinese hinterland that many thought

Left: *Chinese infants go through a standard kung fu routine to promote health and vitality before school. All kung fu practice on mainland China today is termed wu shu (war arts), although it does not resemble the battlefield skills of the past.*

Left: *Wu shu performer displaying his dexterity and control in the use of rope darts. Used correctly, this long-range weapon can be put to devastating effect in unseating mounted horsemen.*

Right: *These two fighters, both in their seventies, perhaps give credence to that proposal that martial arts promote longevity. Skill and form are more important than ferocity.*

Left: *Liang Yiquan, a shaolin boxing teacher, demonstrates the long-tassel spear, once an important weapon of Chinese foot soldiers.*

Right: *Liu Zhiqing, one of the oldest kung fu instructors in mainland China today, coaches one of his pupils in broadsword play. This type of sword is the biggest in the Chinese arsenal.*

Above: *Sifu Dave Lea adopts the horse-stance posture. A beginner can expect to last three minutes in this position.*

Right: *A tremendous inside flying roundhouse kick from the US forms champion Cynthia Rothrock.*

had long since become obsolete. However, the program was hardly off the ground before it was stopped because of the war with Japan.

Following the Communists' rise to power shortly after World War II, many boxing masters fled the mainland and sought refuge in Hong Kong and Taiwan (then Formosa). This mass exodus brought the northern styles before a new public and the impact was so enormous that it even spread to the West. The present government on mainland China attempted a scientific study to see how kung fu could promote good health among the population, working on the principle that a healthy nation is a prosperous nation. It was at this time that the accepted name of kuo shu reverted back to its original wu shu. Today the People's Republic sends wu shu delegations to all parts of the world, giving demonstrations of their highly gymnastic forms of kung fu. Modern wu shu techniques incorporate about 20 of the old systems in their repertoire.

Training in a kung fu style consists of systematically learning and practicing pre-arranged sets or patterns, known as forms, which simulate various combat situations. Through exercises the student is physically and

psychologically prepared for an actual combat encounter (taken to mean self-defense in a street situation). Training demands absolute discipline, endurance and diligence, if the adept is to master the most skilled techniques.

A prerequisite in some of the traditional schools of kung fu is to strengthen the internal leg muscles, which normally remain inactive, by practicing the *ma pu*, or the horse stance. Horse-stance drills have been practiced throughout kung fu's 1000-year history, the students traditionally had to stand with the legs apart to shoulder width, the buttocks tucked in, and with the back kept straight. The student initially spent 10 minutes in the posture, gradually building up the time to the maximum of half a day. The horse stance is not only important for moving from one stance to another, but is also the primary position for eliciting proper breathing techniques. Besides developing strength, balance, and stamina in the legs and lower body the ma pu posture also tests the student's patience and sincerity.

Kung fu was brought to the West partly by American servicemen returning from South-east Asia after the wars in Japan, Korea, and Vietnam, and partly by second-generation American-Chinese, who revealed their arts, disregarding the age-old laws of secrecy. Their Western counterparts could not comprehend why they should stand with their legs apart practicing deep breathing for hours on end and Eastern discipline could not persuade them of its worth, and they quit training.

Since Bruce Lee and the mass media popularized kung fu exploitation the traditional harsh discipline has been modified, making it a little easier for the Western student to gain proficiency and eventually mastery of the art. When a student asked how long he must remain in a horse stance, a traditional teacher would have replied, 'until the pain stops naturally of its own accord.'

In kung fu training the novice learns that because the upper half of the body controls weaving and evasion tactics, the waist is the important gap between the upper and lower part of the body in controlling the entire body. Breathing high in the chest area raises the center of gravity, while breathing low allows a more stable stance and better control of the body. This is why the lower abdominal region of the body is regarded as the source of all power (the tantien). Strong thighs give power to the legs, thus controlling the rising and

dropping movements involved in kung fu. The hands and feet are the fastest and strongest part of the body, and thus provide the widest range of fighting possibilities. In punching techniques, speed, strength and flexibility are of the utmost importance. The muscles of the shoulders, wrists and hands must be loose in order to generate sufficient power for effective strikes and blocks, unlike many styles of karate where the muscles are locked for maximum impact. Both kung fu and karate achieve the same end, but by different routes.

Although the legs have a longer reach and are more powerful than the arms, they are not as flexible. Because of their bulk, in many kung fu styles they are used for maneuvering. The main striking areas of the few kicks that are employed include the instep, ball of the foot, and the entire heel region. In the styles which do use kicking techniques to some advantage, all kick from the front legs. In karate most kicks are executed off the back leg, using the front leg as a support. Flexibility in kicking techniques is achieved through practicing a special series of stretching exercises. Stretching prepares all of the body's natural weapons for combat.

Traditionally there was no colored-belt grading system in China, it was hastily devised when kung fu became popular in the West to act as an incentive and to satisfy the student's ego. Interestingly, when the student reaches the stage of instructor (black sash standard), interest in belts and grades seems to disappear, and concentration is on learning the central core of the system.

When the student becomes reasonably proficient he is usually eager to test the techniques against his peers. Various schools of martial arts formed a competition circuit to satisfy this urge, first on a regional, but then on a national level. Probably the most famous is the US kempo chief Ed Parker's Long Beach nationals, where at one time or another since its inception every national and world champion first tested their fighting ability. It must be pointed out, however, that modern competition fighting, which incorporates numerous flamboyant techniques, would be totally impractical in a real combat situation, and bears no relationship to the traditional techniques of ancient China.

Kung fu students are taught to defend the Five Shaolin Gates – the head, heart, solar plexus, groin and lungs. An opponent's combat skills and strength can be assessed by his

Above: *An alternative defense-ready posture. The arm extended across the body acts as a barrier which can move either up or down depending upon whether the attack is a punch or kick.*
Top: *A practitioner in the* guard position. The extended fist is prepared to strike, while the open-palm rear guard protects the body from attack.
Right: *A sifu from the choy li fut system of kung fu strikes an attacker with a claw grab to the face.*

response to initial quarter-power attacks, or feints. Once his response has been determined, the student must remember the three A's – assimilate, assess, then attack. Delivery of a well-timed and well-executed strike can mean all the difference between victory and defeat in a fight.

The ultimate prize in martial arts' training requires not just mastery of fighting techniques but the vital cultivation of personal spirituality (a sense of peace, tranquillity and wisdom). This is the essence of all martial arts' training. Whether in training or in real combat, kung fu must be totally instinctive. When the mind is concerned with the opponent's action, or with defeat by the opponent (maybe he is twice your size) one instantly becomes self-captivated and ultimately, self-defeated. The perfection of kung fu is to let the body take over instinctively, without rational thought, enabling the body to respond spontaneously and without conscious effort. When the mind becomes conscious, it ceases to be instinctive. Thus the final goal in kung fu is arriving at the state of 'no-mindness.'

A great many schools of kung fu exist today, with their fighting concepts evolving from observing nature in all her glory. A little over 700 years after the death of Bodhidharma, the monk named Chueh Yuan came to Shaolin Temple. He refined the kung fu system then practiced at the monastery to embrace 72 forms. Li Ch'eng of Shansi province elaborated the 72 forms into 170 distinct actions one hundred years later. These 170 movements are the basis of the present Shaolin boxing systems.

The Shaolin fist forms are divided into five schools, each was established in a particular monastery. They are *o-mei (er-mei), wu-tang, fukien, honan* (origin Shaolin school) and *kuangtung.* In southern China the five basic variations of Shaolin chuan were created by the five original monks who managed to escaped the carnage in 1674 and consequently created their own family systems of Hung, Lau, Mok, Choy and Li.

Choy li fut is one of the more popular styles of kung fu practiced today, being practiced by nearly one million martial arts artists worldwide. This style originated at King Mui village, in the province of Kwangtung. The founder was Chan Heung, who began learning kung fu as a small boy. After training for nearly 10 years he met an old monk, Li Yau Shan, with whom he trained for another 10 years. Retiring to the mountains some years later Heung met a holy man, Choy Fook, who in his earlier years was reputedly one of the best kung fu fighters in China, but who had disappeared without a trace. Heung begged Choy to teach him his style of fighting. The two men lived together in the mountains for eight years, then Choy suddenly died.

Chan Heung stayed in the mountains after his master's death, in order to combine the two fighting systems he had been taught. Heung's subtle refinements created a unique style of combat. He called it choy li fut, taking the names of both his teachers and combining it with the Chinese word fut (Buddha).

The style is characterized by its free-swinging arm movements, long-range punching and wide stances. The fist strikes are quite unusual as they incorporate a series of very fast back fists and uppercuts, employed in a figure-eight motion with the arms swinging about like a windmill. It is this windmill effect, with the practitioner's fists raining down in all directions, that makes this style a little difficult to block and counterattack. There are 29 different forms in choy li fut and 18 weapons sets. One of the most interesting weapons of the system is the nine dragon trident. This spear-like weapon is unique to choy li fut and combines the features of five other weapons. It weighs over 128 pounds and is in excess of eight feet long. The name derives from the razor-sharp hook-like objects at the end of the spear, which resemble dragon's teeth. Because of its bulk and weight very few practitioners ever learn to use it with dexterity although Chan Heung could apparently manipulate the trident so formidably that he could fight off 20 opponents. The founder's original trident is in safe keeping with the head of the present-day grandmaster of choy li fut. Incorporated within the choy li fut system is the original *shih-pa lo-han* set (Buddha's 18-disciple exercise system). A branch or offshoot from choy li fut is *bak sing* (north wind).

When Chan Heung began to teach his art to the local villagers in the 1840s his fame as a great fighter quickly spread far and wide. About this time, a ship was stopped at a place called Tiger Gate, where Chinese officials discovered that it was carrying a large quantity of opium. It was immediately ordered to be burned, so starting the Opium Wars.

The war spread along the Pearl River and caused much destruction to the villages, including Chan Heung's. Great anti-British feeling was fostered, and the young men of the surrounding countryside staged a revolt, with Chan Heung as their leader. The shortage of

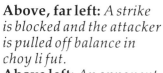

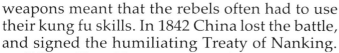

Above, far left: *A strike is blocked and the attacker is pulled off balance in choy li fut.*
Above left: *An opponent is sent to the floor with a short claw strike to the eyes.*

Above: *The classic praying mantis posture.*
Above right: *A fist strike is about to be intercepted with a double-palm grab.*
Right: *A praying mantis sifu with hooking claws ready to strike.*

weapons meant that the rebels often had to use their kung fu skills. In 1842 China lost the battle, and signed the humiliating Treaty of Nanking.

When Chan Heung returned home with his men he felt ashamed of betraying his Buddhist faith by bearing arms against his fellow men. Yet when it was explained to him that he had merely protected his family in the face of danger, his guilt subsided.

Five years later trouble erupted again, when the secret triad society known as the Hung League led the Taiping revolt. Their war cry was 'overthrow the Ch'ing and restore the Ming.' This time Chan Heung refused to fight, so he travelled south with his family, setting up kung fu schools along the way.

In 1864 he went to the United States, and stayed in San Francisco for five years. While he was there he was appointed martial arts instructor for Chinatown. Returning home some years later, he found that his choy li fut organization had grown to quite epic proportions. Chan Heung died peacefully in 1875, but his style lives on in all parts of the world.

One of the most unusual styles of kung fu is the praying mantis. This mantis is a grasshopper-like insect, but much smaller. A northern style, its full title is *tong long* or *tang lang chuan*. This style features stabbing- and ripping-hand maneuvers, incorporating quick

and decisive body turns. Pinpoint precision and accuracy is required from its adherents in combat. The practioner makes his hands resemble the claw of a praying mantis, then in lightening-fast moves the adept jabs at the adversaries' vital spots, such as the eyes and throat. The principal maneuver of the system is to grab an opponent by hooking one of his limbs with the claw-like hand to expose a vital part upon his body to a strike. Although basically a northern sil lum system, many variations on the theme exist in both north and south China. All the stances are short, and when attacking a quick sideways stepping motion is implemented. One of the many variations in existence is the seven stars mantis, which is apparently based upon the Chinese theory of heavenly constellations.

When moving in to attack, a praying-mantis stylist moves both his feet and hands at the same time. The style requires that attacks are carried out with extreme speed and excellent co-ordination. Two of the finest practitioners teaching in America today are sifus Chan Poi and Brendan Lai.

The praying-mantis style originated at the now-legendary Shaolin Temple about 350 years ago. Wong Long, a student, was continually being beaten in friendly sparring matches with the other monks and try as he would, Wong Long could never seem to match the proficiency and expertise of his peers.

The only recourse left open to him was to retire to meditate on his faults. During one of these meditative sessions, he observed two insects engaged in a fierce battle for survival. One was a praying mantis, the other was a cicada (a type of grasshopper). Although the mantis was a lot smaller and lighter than the cicada, it was moving around in a very definite pattern, striking out with its claw-like talon then quickly withdrawing. Attacking from both sides, the mantis totally confused the cicada, and it flew away, beaten.

Wong Long was so fascinated that he captured the mantis and took it home with him. He spent many hours prodding the mantis with a blade of bamboo grass, observing its every reaction to the intended attack. Wong Long wrote down his observations, noting particularly that the mantis could hook with its claw in every direction. After a year or more devising a system based on his detailed notes and adapting the movements to suit the human form, Wong Long put his theories to the test. He

Left: *Master Brendan Lai of San Francisco is exercising a balance posture from the praying mantis system of kung fu. Note his hands, which assume the shape of a claw.*

Above: *The late grandmaster of hung gar, Lam Sai Wing demonstrates a knife form from the system. Forms or sets familiarize the practitioner with the movements when training alone.*

Above: *Lam Sai Wing (seated) and the present teacher of hung gar, Master Chan Han Chung of Hong Kong. Hung gar is also known as hung kune or the Fist of Hung.*

Below: *An old master and his student work out. The young student attacks with a cranes-beak strike, but it is intercepted by the old man who blocks with an inside forearm and prepares to counterstrike with a tiger claw.*

returned to the monastery and systematically fought and beat every monk there. In celebration of his success the abbot of Shaolin named the fighting style after Tong Long.

Hung gar is a style of kung fu that is as popular as choy li fut. It is an original Shaolin style, whose methods are based on the five animals. Although the ma pu stance is seen in many kung fu styles, it is to hung gar we must look for the exact interpretation of the stance. It is said that because of the persecution of boxers by the Ch'ing dynasty hung gar students had to train in strict secrecy. Students of this southern-style family system had to resort to training in the sampans and junks that crowded the busy waterfront areas of southern China's ports. The low roofs prevented practitioners from standing erect, so they had to adopt a very low horse stance when training.

Left: *Sifu Dave Lea in the crane stance. One of the five animals of hung gar, in the crane system the fingers form the shape of a crane's beak. The fingers can then be used for hooking and striking at the soft or fleshy parts of the body such as the eyes.*

Above: *The Chinese instructor or sifu walks up and down his class to ensure that his young students are correctly positioned in the horse stance, and are executing their punching techniques in the right manner.*

Right: *Youngsters develop their kicking power on hand-held pads.*
Below right: *The outside temple walls in Fatshan, where wing chun kung fu pioneer, the late grandmaster Yip Man, lived.*

Hung meaning, 'to stand tall with integrity,' and gar, meaning 'family or clan,' is a very hard external system based upon an adaptation of the Shaolin tiger style. Hung combined his tiger style with his wife's white crane style to create a formidable kung fu that allegedly has a thrust punch that always results in a knockout. To become fully proficient in the system takes at least eight years. Although a hung gar practitioner specializes in the tiger and crane forms, there are also elements of the dragon, leopard and snake style.

Wing chun kung fu is probably the best known of all the kung fu styles, and the most widely practiced, largely because of the late Bruce Lee, who trained in this devastating kung fu system as a youth. Wing chun provided a basis for Lee's own eclectic style, *Jeet kune do* (Way of the Intercepting Fist).

Wing chun is the only style created by a woman. Many martial artists believe it is the most lethal of all the kung fu forms, and is often referred to as 'Hong Kong street fighting.' Wing chun is a very practical and scientific method of combat that cares little for the niceties of fair play and good taste. Its one aim is to wipe out an attack lethally the second it is initiated. The art has no superfluous techniques, nor does it embrace a myriad of different weapons. Although invented 400 years ago the system needs no modernizing in the twentieth century. The art is quick, effective and produces instant results.

Wing chun was invented by Ng Mui, a Buddhist nun at the Shaolin Temple, who was one of the few survivors to escape the sacking of the Shaolin Temple by the Ching troops. Ng Mui fled to a temple in Tai Leung Shan, where she continued to train in her style of kung fu, *mui fa chuan* (plum flower fist). During her frequent trips to the local village Ng Mui befriended the daughter of a beancurd seller, Yim Wing Chun. One day she found the girl in tears because the local gangster wanted her for his concubine. Feeling sorry for the girl, Ng Mui told her to tell the gangster to wait six months, then she would come to him willingly. The gangster agreed to the terms.

During that time Ng Mui taught Yim Wing Chun her plum flower style, plus a few added refinements she had introduced since being on the run from the sacked Shaolin Temple. Six months later the gangster came for Yim Wing Chun, who told him that if he wanted her, he would have to prove himself by fighting and beating her. Sensing an easy victory, the gangster laughingly agreed. Within seconds of the fight commencing the gangster was on the ground with a broken nose and arm, plus three ribs broken into the bargain. He crawled away in pain never to be seen again. As the years passed Yim Wing Chun married, but always continued to train. As she became competent in kung fu, Yim found that there were certain areas within the art that needed some subtle refining. She felt that the plum flower fist was a little too complex and placed too much reliance on power techniques and strong horse stances, more befitting a man than a woman.

She eventually evolved a system of fighting that was neither complicated nor strenuous, but retained maximum efficiency. She dedicated her new style to the nun who had first taught her, but named it after herself (the name Wing Chun means beautiful springtime). At a later date the only two weapons in the system were introduced. The first was the *pak charn dao* (butterfly knives), which refers to the eight

cutting blades and eight basic cutting movements of these twin knives. The second weapon is the six-and-a-half-point-pole *(luk-dim-boun-kwan)*. This pole was invented by a Shaolin monk named Gee-Sin and measures about eight feet in length.

The wing chun family tree is so accurate that the masters of the art can be traced back nearly 400 years right from the style's inception to contemporary masters such as the late grandmaster Yip Man. He lived in the city of Fatshan on the Chinese mainland, but during the Communist takeover fled the city to live in Hong Kong. Here he set up his kwoon (training club) and began to teach wing chun. Wing chun was then new to the kung fu fighters of Hong Kong and many flocked to learn this devastating art.

By the early 1960s Yip Man revealed his secret art to the modern world, although he still would not teach anyone who was not pure Chinese. Of his many great students of that era, some have gone on to become great masters in their own right, including masters such as Leung Ting, Wong Shun Leung, and William Cheung. As in most of the martial arts, once a student has become proficient in the system he goes his own way and interprets it to suit his own personality. In this way, all the arts are constantly evolving.

Wing chun began to change the moment ex-students left Hong Kong. Each student taught in a different way to the other; these revisions have created enormous conflicts in the kung fu world for the last 15 years, with the top instructors vying for positions of power.

In 1970 the grandmaster Yip Man contracted throat cancer, which eventually spread to his stomach. An operation failed to stem the disease. Knowing that his days were numbered, Yip Man left his sickbed, his body racked with pain, his lifeforce all but gone, to make an eight-millimeter movie of his techniques. He included all the forms and the wooden-dummy techniques to be preserved for posterity in their purest form. Upon his death in 1972 his son, Yip Chun, became the world grandmaster of wing chun.

Foreigners were taught the kung fu system after Bruce Lee's films – featuring some amazing fighting sequences – created a surge of enthusiasm in the West. It is because of Bruce Lee that the popularity of kung fu and the martial arts in general spread worldwide.

All wing chun training starts with the

Left: *Sifu Samuel Kwok, a student of the current grandmaster of wing chun, practices with butterfly knives.*

Above: *Sifu Austin Goh, in a classic wing chun front-guard position, delivers a low kick with the heel of his foot.*

learning of *siu lim tao* (little idea form). This teaches the student the use of the hand movements and the basic stances. The simplicity of the wing chun system is evident from the fact that there are just three forms to learn. They are *siu lim tao, chum kui* (searching for the bridge) and finally *bil jee* (stabbing fingers). This last form is taught only after the student has mastered the application of the first two forms. During the training of bil jee, the student is taught to attack the vital points of an opponent. At this stage the practitioner has reached the highest proficiency and becomes free from all restrictions and rules, and can therefore be unpredictable in a fight.

A training aid of the wing chun system that has become famous worldwide, is that of *chi sau* (sticking hands). This is a training method rather than a method for actual fighting. It is used for developing the sensitivity of the arms, so that the practitioner can feel the opponent's intentions and moves. Chi sau teaches correct elbow positioning and how to defend oneself with the minimum motion or effort. Correct application of chi sau can control the movements of an opponent. There are no set positions in chi sau; the aim is to attack from all angles and the opponent has to counter immediately and redirect his own attack.

Even the most junior student must understand the importance and usage of chi sau in wing chun, because chi sau is the bridge between the forms and fighting techniques. The exercise is compulsory in the system and no student can learn the sparring techniques without first having acquired a good basic knowledge of chi sau.

When beginning this exercise the student first starts off with *dan chi* (single stick hand). Single hand is a fixed set of movements with no

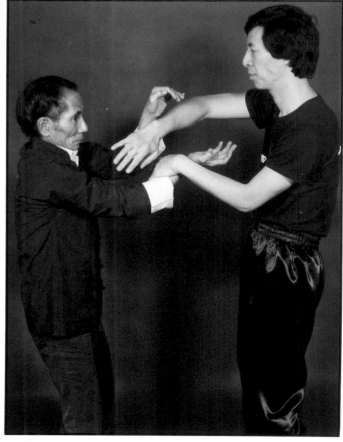

changes, it is only for the basic preparation of double-hand chi sau. In dan chi there are only six moves, three are executed by one student who faces the other practicing the corresponding sequence. Dan chi emphasizes the student's sensitivity to the changing energy of a partner. Each movement should be 'felt,' it should be deliberate, but relaxed, not using strength. The practitioners do not actually try to hit each other but rather appreciate their partner's changes.

From dan chi the practitioner moves to double sticking hands. In chi sau it is not strength against strength, it is only by an opponent making a mistake that one can strike. At the advanced stage of the exercise, when both partners have gained the 'feeling,' the finer subtleties of wing chun come into their own. Each partner then has to try to lure the other into making a wrong move so that he can find an opening to strike.

When using the fighting technique of wing chun the primary aim is to guard the 'centerline,' an imaginary line running from the top of the skull down to the groin area. It is said that this area houses all the vital points on the human anatomy. Because even wing chun fighters exert the minimum amount of force to do the maximum amount of work they have more stamina than most other fighters. This 'economy of motion,' as practitioners call it, makes the art especially suitable for women.

There are only eight kicks in the system, which are all short ranged and aimed below the waist. When delivered correctly they are almost impossible to defend against. In defending the centerline, students are taught never to present the opponent with a frontal target, but to turn sideways, thus reducing the target area by more than 50 percent.

Another wing chun training device is the *mook jong* (wooden dummy), which resembles a human opponent. In the wing chun system practice on the wooden dummy constitutes the final stage of instructions. Some 108 traditional hand techniques can be practiced on the seven sections of mook jong, although in recent times they have been increased to 116. It is thought that the mook jong is a relic from the time of the Shaolin Temple; other kung fu styles, such as hung gar, also make frequent use of a similar device. Wooden dummy training plays an important part in the development of wing chun hand techniques, and also helps to toughen up and harden the limbs.

Above: *Master and student at work. Samuel Kwok teaching the finer points of attack and defense.*
Left: *Yip Chun and Samuel Kwok practice the famous hand exercise of wing chun, chi sau (sticking hands).*

Far left, top: *Sifu Samuel Kwok tests his wing chun technique on the training device known as the wooden man or dummy.*
Top left: *The current master of wing chun, grandmaster Yip Chun, demonstrates how to block a punch while simultaneously executing a palm-strike to the jaw.*

Above: *Grandmaster Dr Leung Ting of Hong Kong, the head of the wing tsun system. Wing tsun is a modified version of wing chun. This master has one of the largest followings in the world.*
Far right: *The man that began it all: the late Bruce Lee in a still from his most successful movie in the West,* Enter the Dragon.

The most notable part of the mook jong is the inverted L-shaped piece which is supposed to resemble a man's leg from the lower thighs downward. Although dummies are now manufactured in factories, dedicated followers of the art will scour the countryside looking for the tree branch that most resembles a leg, paying particular attention to the 'knee cap.' There are stories about keen students breaking their own limbs by falling from trees in an attempt to secure the perfect branch to make their mook jong.

Undoubtedly the man who had the largest influence on the martial arts in recent times, perhaps even of the twentieth century, was Bruce Lee, the little dragon. Film star, choreographer, martial artist and master of jeet kune do, Lee was a man ahead of his time. Arguably, only today is he being fully understood.

Bruce Lee was born on 27 November 1940 in the year of and at the hour of the Dragon (7-9pm) at San Francisco's Chinese Hospital to Hoi Chuen and Grace Li. He was fourth of five children, Peter, Agnes, Phoebe, Bruce and Robert. Hoi Li was a Chinese opera performer and was appearing in New York while his wife was staying with friends in San Francisco. They named their new son Jun Fan (return to San Francisco) because Grace Li felt that one day he would return to his birthplace, but later on he was renamed Yuen Kam (small Phoenix). Usually this was a girl's name, but it was given to confuse evil spirits. It was the supervising doctor Mary Glover, who gave him the nick-name Bruce which was used later, after he anglisized Li to Lee.

A few months after Bruce was born the Lis returned to Hong Kong, where the humid atmosphere made the new addition to the family very ill. In fact Bruce was sickly throughout early childhood, a very different person from the future star of Hollywood. He began his film career through his father's friends and connections in the profession. His first screen appearance, when he was three months old, was in the movie *Golden Gate Girl*. By the time he was 18 years old Bruce had appeared in more than 20 films, in parts from a street urchin to a teenage rebel in such films as *Kid Cheung* and *Orphan*. He was such a hit in the latter that audiences nicknamed him 'Little Dragon,' a name which stuck throughout his teenage and adult career.

With such a claim to fame at an early age it seems odd that he took to roaming the streets with gangs, and was constantly getting involved in fights. About this time, when Bruce was aged about thirteen, it occured to him that he may be at a disadvantage if he was ever caught alone by another gang. He decided to learn how to take care of himself by learning a martial art. He had already practiced tai chi chuan with his father but the art needs many years of serious training before a student is proficient enough to defend himself. Bruce decided that he needed a style with more immediate results. He had tried a few different styles of kung fu but none seemed to fit the bill. Bruce eventually settled on wing chung; the system can be learned more immediately and is also more applicable to defense on the street. At first his interest in the art was only as a street-fighting technique, but under the instruction of Yip Man, instructors and senior students, such as Wong Shun Leung and William Cheung, Bruce progressed in the art, though he never learned the complete wing chun system.

The street confrontations continued, and there were often illegal contests (*kong sau* bouts) between different kung fu classes, which occasionally led to trouble with the police. One day he was held in the police station after a contest, and Mrs Li had to collect him from jail. She gave him a strict warning that it had to stop, or she would tell his father. Though he loved and respected his father, Bruce also feared him and he agreed to his mother's demand. His mother suggested that Bruce, now 18, should go to America and claim his right of US citizenship. With $100 in his pocket Bruce made the journey which would

change his life. Later Bruce admitted that if the decision had not been made he might have ended up in serious trouble.

In Seattle he lived in a room above the restaurant of Mrs Ruby Chow, in return for working as a waiter for her, and decided to finish his education, which he had neglected in Hong Kong. He enrolled at the Edison Technical High School, and worked hard at maths, science, history and philosophy, and after gaining his high school diploma went to the University of Washington. Among the subjects he studied were English and philosophy, as well as sports related to movement such as gymnastics and wrestling and the martial arts. Bruce found time to continue practicing wing chun and also taught a few of his friends.

Above: *A poster advertising Bruce Lee's great movie* Enter the Dragon.
Left: *Bruce Lee in action. Karate practitioners were usually the bad guys in his films.*
Above right: *The fist that shook the world: a film poster of Lee's movie* Fist of Fury.
Right: *Bruce Lee exhibiting his tremendous kicking ability. This side kick to the head was typical of Lee's method of fighting in the movies.*

Although he was still only a young man he had established such a large reputation in the martial arts fraternity that fighters from various styles came to see him, to find out who he was and what all the fuss was about. Experienced men from judo, jujitsu, karate, and the then almost unheard of kung fu found his speed and economy of movement unbelievable. Some even changed their style in order to study with him. At first Bruce taught on the back lot of Ruby Chow's restaurant and then anywhere he could find room – in car parks, basements, and college campuses. It was during one of these classes that Bruce met his future wife, Linda Emery.

In 1964 two things happened which were to change his life. He married Linda and decided to quit university and teach kung fu full time to earn a living. Times were hard at first but gradually it started to pay off. The second major event was a confrontation with the Chinese community of San Francisco, who sent a delegation to Bruce's school on Broadway in Oakland. There are two versions of what happened: according to his wife Linda Lee, the group objected to Bruce teaching non-Chinese students (at that time there was an unwritten rule that only Chinese should study kung fu). They gave Bruce an ultimatum to stop teaching non-Chinese or meet their champion in a challenge match. Bruce could agree, or fight! If he lost then tradition dictated that he would have to close down his school.

Bruce accepted the challenge from the delegation's champion, a man called Jack Man Wong, a *my jong law horn* kung fu stylist. According to Linda Lee and Dan Inosanto (Bruce Lee's friend and student), Bruce beat Wong with little trouble and threw the delegation out of his school.

The other version of the story, as told by Wong years after Lee's death, was that the match was only a friendly one, in which rules were agreed (no open-hand strikes, such as finger attacks to the eyes were allowed). But even though Bruce broke these rules the match finished as a draw. Whichever version is the truth, one thing is sure, Bruce felt that wing chun kung fu, even though it is supposed to be a 'modern stripped down style' was still restricting. He thought that the fight should have been over in less than the eleven minutes it had taken, and he was surprised that he was out of breath at the end of it. He decided that he had to adapt what he knew, to develop a new style.

Bruce Lee had already made slight changes to his wing chun style but after the Jack Man Wong challenge he began assimilating all the knowledge he could amass from each and every fighting style he could discover. He researched every style possible either through books or by training with martial arts masters and instructors. He sought the advice of his friends in the martial arts, including Ed Parker (kempo, karate), Wally Jay (jujitsu), Jesse Glover (judo), Dan Inosanto (karate, kempo, escrima) and Taky Kiura (judo). Bruce Lee's new style became known as *jun fan* (his own name at birth) but as time went on he changed it for a term which encapsulated his views on combat: *jeet kune do* (jeet – intercepting, kune – fist, do – way or style). 'The way of the intercepting fist' was born.

Fifty percent of the style was based upon wing chun, but he included techniques and ideas and principles from kung fu, karate, judo, jujitsu, aikido, la savate, boxing, wrestling, muay thai, escrima and even the 'dirty techniques' of street fighting. Over the years Bruce and his leading students developed and polished his ideas into a modern, unorthodox combat style.

Usually 'style' denotes a set way of teaching and learning, passed on through the years from instructor to pupil in exactly the same way. Lee, however, thought everyone was an individual and should tailor their way of fighting to suit themselves, not just imitate their instructors. He encouraged students to experiment with various styles, and absorb from them what is useful for their size and build, to finish up with a type of free-style form. Consequently one person's form will be different from the next, even though they may have studied the same styles or had the same instructor. This was Bruce Lee's individual jeet kune do.

Despite proving his theories in contest most instructors of traditional systems thought he was a young upstart who did not know what he was talking about and that his jeet kune do was nothing more than glorified street fighting. Yet many martial artists, some of them world-recognized figures such as Ed Parker, Wally Jay, Dan Inosanto, Leo Fong (kung fu, boxing), Al Dacoscas (kung fu, escrima) and Jhoon Rhee (taekwondo), acknowledged his skill and foresight. Sport karate fighters also went to Bruce Lee for special training, including Joe Lewis, who retired as the undefeated heavyweight champion, Mike Stone, the undefeated light-

Above: *Bruce Lee in a scene from* Big Boss. *The famous side-on pose was* *his hallmark, and had audiences the world over cheering in the aisles.*

heavyweight champion, and Chuck Norris, who was US/World champion seven times in his long career.

Bruce Lee was not only a martial artist or a fighter but also a very articulate young man. He appeared on television and radio chat shows and wrote excellent articles for martial art magazines, such as the prestigious *Black Belt* magazine in America and in 1963 wrote a book called *Chinese Kung Fu: The Philosophical Art of Self-Defence*. Although Bruce was always scribbling down notes and ideas nothing else was published until after his death. Four volumes were compiled using photographs taken for his intended book entitled *Bruce Lee's Fighting Method* and a book which he only intended for his students, *Tao of Jeet Kune Do*. This is really a collection of his thoughts and drawings, from which only an experienced martial artist could grasp any significance. Had he lived it would undoubtedly have been a fantastic account of all his ideas and theories.

While Lee was striving to perfect his own form of combat he was also burning to realize his greatest ambition – to be an actor, to achieve super stardom, to be the first Chinese actor to gain world recognition and to show kung fu on the screen as it really is. Luck was to play a big part in his road to fame. He attended Ed Parker's 1964 International Karate Championships at Long Beach, California, where he performed a demonstration which Ed Parker filmed. Also there was Jay Sebring, a Hollywood hairstylist, who mentioned Lee to William Dozier, a producer who at the time was looking for someone to play Charlie Chan's number one son in a new television series. After seeing Parker's film of Bruce in action Dozier contacted Lee. The Charlie Chan series was scrapped before it was started, but Dozier was casting for the series *Green Hornet*, an adult version of the successful *Batman* series. Bruce was cast as the hero's servant and side kick Kato. Though it only ran 26 episodes Bruce received good reviews, particularly for his kung fu skills.

With some good reviews under his belt Bruce expected offers to come flooding in, but

nothing happened. One producer told him nothing big would come his way, he would never become a star because he was Chinese. Bruce could not accept that. Bruce was now teaching many celebrities jeet kune do, including James Coburn, James Garner, Steve McQueen, script writer Sterling Silliphant, director Roman Polanski, and Joe Hyams, writer and husband of actress Elke Sommer. Some of them tried to help Bruce find work getting him on *Ironside* and into four episodes of *Longstreet*, about a blind detective. Probably his best minor film role was as Winslow Wong in *Marlowe* (1969) which starred his film star pupil James Garner and was written by friend and pupil Sterling Silliphant.

Again, despite good reviews, star roles continued to evade him. He was considered for the starring role in a series called *Warrior*, but it was shelved. Later on the program was resurrected and renamed *Kung Fu*, starring dancer/actor David Carradine. Lee was supposedly dropped because it was thought he looked too Chinese for the part of a Shaolin monk. The second project to fall through was written by Lee, Coburn and Silliphant; the main character was to be played by James Coburn and Bruce was to portray five different characters. They offered the script, which tackled the philosophical side of the martial arts, to Warner

Brothers who accepted it, but there was one drawback. The film had to be made in India to use up Warner's money which was 'blocked' there. The three men went over to scout for locations and native fighters but with little luck. Finally the plan fell through. (In 1978 David Carradine acquired the rights, and made a praiseworthy attempt with Jeff Cooper taking Coburn's role, and Carradine playing four roles.)

In 1970 Bruce paid a visit to Hong Kong (the first time since 1965 when he had returned for his father's funeral), and was surprised at the marvellous welcome he received. Unknown to him the *Green Hornet* series had been running in Hong Kong and he had become a star without knowing it. At that time Raymond Chow, a former member of one of Hong Kong's major studios, had set up his own studio called Golden Harvest. Chow saw his chance and contacted Lee. Shaw Brothers were also trying to lure Bruce, but their offer was only a standard (junior) actor's contract. Chow offered Bruce $7500 per film and the chance of star roles. It was good money by Hong Kong standards and Bruce Lee finally joined Golden Harvest.

Lee's first film with them, *Big Boss* (entitled *Fist of Fury* in the United States), was made in Thailand in 1971. Filming was difficult. The original director was sacked and replaced by Lo

Above left: *A flying somersault kick from* Enter the Dragon. *Lee, apart from being a brilliant martial artist, was also super fit.*

Above: *Bruce Lee has struck his opponent under the chin with a double kick, and somersaults in the air to arrive feet first on the ground.*

Wei. Bruce had to rewrite a lot of the poor script. Bruce and Lo Wei did not get on, partly because Lo listened to the racing on the radio during filming. However, when it was released *Big Boss* smashed Hong Kong's box-office record, previously held by *The Sound of Music* and took $3.5 million within 19 days, and then smashed records throughout the world. Later in 1971 Bruce made his second film, *Fists of Fury* (retitled *Chinese Connection* in the United States). The film was based loosely on a true story and demonstrated the use of the nunchaku and included a foreign fighter (Bob Baker as a Russian) in the plot. Within 13 days *Fists of Fury* surpassed its predecessor's record by taking $4½ million. With its traditional anti-Japanese theme and Bruce's 'We (Chinese) are not the sick men of Asia' line it could not help but be a big hit in Hong Kong and the East. Bruce Lee was now a national hero.

For his third film in 1972, Lee decided to go it alone with *Way Of The Dragon* (*Return of the Dragon* in the United States). He set up his own studio, Concorde, under the Golden Harvest

banner, and practically made the film himself, starring, directing, producing, casting, choosing the costumes and locations, and choreographing the fight scenes. It was the first Hong Kong film to be shot on location in Europe (Rome) and, as with the earlier two films, broke all box-office records. Bruce had predicted that it would make more than $5 million to a chorus of disbelief from the critics who laughed on the other side of their faces when *Way of the Dragon* surpassed even Lee's predictions. Again he used the nunchaku, this time two sets (censored in Britain), and three foreign fighters: Wong In-Sik, Bob Wall and, in the memorable fight scene in the Rome Colosseum, seven times US world champion Chuck Norris. Western critics called the film amateurish, but it must be remembered that it was Lee's first attempt at directing and, like his first two films, was not intended for release in the West. These films were aimed at an Eastern audience to make Lee's name.

Riding on the success of his third box-office smash Lee now decided to make a film featuring some of the world's best martial artists showing how people can adapt different fighting styles. The title was *Game of Death* and the story line was simple – a national treasure is stolen and placed on the top floor of a five-story pagoda on an island near Korea. Outside is a group of fighters led by a large hulk-shaped man, while each floor of the pagoda is guarded by a defender. The final floor of the pagoda was protected by a seven-foot four-inch fighter who uses a non-style, much like Bruce's own jeet kune do. After some initial shooting everything came to a stop when Warner's came up with an offer Lee could not refuse: a starring role in the first American martial arts film as well as complete control over the fight scenes. It was what he had been waiting for. Recently his films had been playing in the West and doing terrific business. Now was the time to conquer America and the rest of the world.

The film Warner's had to offer Bruce was *Blood and Steel*, later retitled *Enter the Dragon*, which co-starred American actor John Saxon. The critics said it was nothing more than a second-rate *Bond* film, yet audiences packed cinemas worldwide to see what is now regarded as the best example of this genre. Various martial artists and martial arts actors were signed up, including Shek Kin (Mr Han), Yang Sie (Bolo), Bob Wall (O'Hara), Jim Kelly (Williams) and Angela Mao (Bruce's sister in a flashback). Bruce Lee also used a variety of weapons, the nunchaku, staff and escrima sticks (all censored in Britain), which he had learned to use with his friend Dan Inosanto. It would be an understatement to say that Lee was very satisfied with the film and expected it to be his biggest to date. Unfortunately he never saw its success.

While *Enter the Dragon* was awaiting release, Bruce resumed work on *Game of Death* but time did not allow him to complete it. Earlier, on 10 May 1973 while dubbing the sound and dialogue for *Enter the Dragon*, he collapsed. By the time Lee was rushed to hospital he was having difficulties breathing. The doctors fought to save his life and, though it was touch and go, finally succeeded. They considered various possible causes – overwork, kidney malfunction, but the most likely was a cerebal oedema, a swelling of the fluid which presses on the brain. When Lee was well again he had a complete check-up by the best doctors in America, who could find nothing wrong with him. In fact they told the 32-year-old star that he had the body of an 18 year old!

On 20 July Lee went with producer Raymond Chow to visit the home of actress and friend Betty Ting Pei to discuss a part for her in *Game of Death*. While there Lee complained of a headache and went to lie down. Chow agreed to meet him later at a restaurant when they were to have talks with Bond star George Lazenby over a major role in the same film. But, when Betty later went to wake Lee she could not get any response. She telephoned for Chow to come round and when he too was unable to stir Lee, he called a doctor. An ambulance rushed Lee to hospital where this time doctors could not revive him. The 'fittest man in the world' was dead. The world was astounded.

There have been many theories explaining Lee's death, which include suicide by gun or overdose, being killed by jealous kung fu masters, and being killed by an expert in the secret art of dim mak, the delayed death touch. It has even been suggested that he had accidentally invoked ill luck and evil spirits in using the word 'death' in his films. It was further suggested that Lee had gone into hiding to escape the triads.

The official autopsy, carried out by the British Home Office (such was the importance given to Bruce Lee), revealed that his brain had swollen like a sponge, weighing 1575 grams instead of the normal 1400 grams. Another coroner, specially sent out to Hong Kong to carry out an independent report, confirmed the finding – death from a brain oedema caused by hypersensitivity to one of the two compounds in the equagesic headache tablet Betty had given him. Death by misadventure was returned. The great man was finally laid to rest, but his influence lives on. Even now his theories, ideas and concepts are only just being understood by martial artists.

One of the most interesting types of kung fu is simian or monkey boxing, better known as *ta sheng men*. It consists of only five sets or patterns, with each set depicting a different principle of movement. The five sets are: the lost monkey, the stone monkey, wooden monkey, tall monkey and drunken monkey. Each set is based on the actions of a monkey meeting a different set of combative circumstances. Because orthodox ta sheng men style only attacks parts of the body below the chest the style was merged with pi kua men, a northern style that later found popularity in southern China. Pi kua men style uses fist strikes, held above the head, to the head and neck of an opponent.

Ta sheng men is also called the great sage style after the monkey king – in the Chinese folk novel *Hsi Yo Chi* – who in a brash moment visited heaven and pompously proclaimed

Right: *Master Chan Sau Chung performs the monkey style, one of the most colorful systems in kung fu. A fighter executes a series of rolling maneuvers, which confuses the opponent. The monkey fighter will then shoot out a kick or punch which catches his adversary completely unawares and which he cannot counter.*
Below right: *Master Chan crouches in a monkey boxer attack position.*

himself the great sage equal to heaven and earth. In the folk tale monkey (real name was Sun Wu-K'ung) was acting as a bodyguard to the Buddhist monk who was searching China for the precious *Tripitaka* scriptures. This tale is based on a real-life transmission of Sanskrit doctrines which furthered the development of Buddhism in China.

Although pi kua men is the older of the two styles ta sheng men is the more famous of the two. It was founded by Kou Sze during the early years of the Chinese republic (1911-49). Kou Sze had been imprisoned on a self-defense murder charge for eight years. Only because he had killed in self-defense did Kou Sze avoid the death sentence. His cell window faced a hillside where a colony of monkeys lived. One day, while he was devotedly going through some of his kung fu techniques in the grand earth style, he saw the monkeys come out and start to fight, he was fascinated by the way they used their speed and agility. Some of the moves they made appeared to be very crafty and sneaky. Kou Sze catalogued their many movements and then incorporated them into his own training regime. In addition to their clever maneuvers, Kou Sze noted their strategem of seeming to retreat but really enticing an opponent into a well-prepared countertrap. By the end of his sentence Kou Sze had perfected his new system of kung fu.

Left: *Two kung fu practitioners engage in staff fighting. The pole usually measures about six feet six inches in length.*
Right: *Doc Fai Wong employs the Chinese fan. A very formidable weapon, in ancient times it was constructed out of thin metal strips.*
Below: *The chain whip is used in this defense against the six-foot pole.*

Upon leaving prison he went to visit his old friend who was a master of pi kua men, but discovered that he had recently died. His friend's son offered to put up Kou Sze until he found somewhere more permanent and in return Kou Sze taught him the complete monkey system. Ken Ten-hai and Kou Sze became great friends, until Kou Sze's death.

Ken Ten-hai then merged the monkey style with his own pi kua men style. He travelled south to propogate the two systems of kung fu. Interestingly, he openly taught his own style of pi kua men but jealously guarded the secret of ta sheng men, teaching it only to a select number of disciples. Today the grandmaster of the style is Chan Sau Chung, who lives in Hong Kong. To ensure the finest quality of Monkey Boxing, students must first learn pi kua men before they can learn ta sheng men.

The monkey techniques of the great sage style consist of mastering the five sets. Students develop power and body toughening through the dictates of the stone monkey set. Long-range attacks are culled from the tall monkey set. Wooden monkey teaches the sneaky tactics and tricks involved in combat, plus the retreats and counters. The lost monkey set deals with defense when the fighter is under pressure.

The last set the drunken monkey is quite amusing to watch. It is based upon the actions of a monkey which stole some wine and be-

came drunk. The fighting techniques teach the student to stagger and lurch around as if drunk, coupled with nimble and erratic steps. The steps have a broken rhythm and are extremely evasive and deceptive, and the unorthodox, awkward movement often baffles and confuses most other kung fu stylists, who are then hesitant, and unprepared for sudden unpredictable attacks or retreats. The staggering body motion and stepping affords the monkey stylist an unorthodox but effective method of eluding thrusts and kicks which he can dodge or, if struck, simply roll with the blow.

A student of ta sheng men has to adopt the behavior and mannerisms of a monkey to understand the principles behind the art. It can be quite a surprise for a new student in a kung fu kwoon to see martial artists jumping up and down and screeching like a monkey.

Bok hok pai, the system of the White Crane, was invented by the Tibetan lamas. It received royal patronage and was reserved solely for the the emperor's hand-picked bodyguard. The style has many secret maneuvers, which were preserved for centuries until the masters recently opened their doors to Western students.

The style originated in northern China when a lama was meditating on a hillside until distracted by a noise. Looking up, he saw the commotion was a fight between a white crane and a fierce ape. The ape was rushing in and

Far left: *Two bok hok pai practitioners fighting with the long pole, balanced on the mui fa joong or plum blossom poles. Fighting on these poles develops a heightened sense of balance. This modern arrangement prevents injury, should practitioners fall.*

Left: *Wah Lum master Chan Poi adopts a pose while delicately balanced on the poles.*
Right: *Keith Hirabashi executes a tremendous leap as he attacks with the three-sectioned staff against a pole fighter.*

attacking the bird, but the crane evaded these brash charges and retaliated with its wings and claws. The battle lasted for quite a time and the lama looked on with great interest. Suddenly the ape turned and fled back into the forest, blinded in one eye. The lama began to emulate the movements of the bird in an attempt to re-create the scene. He stood on one leg and kicked out hard with the other, just as the crane had done. Eventually the lama formulated eight different techniques based upon what he had witnessed, incorporating all the natural movements used by the crane and adding to them some of the ape's footwork techniques and grabbing maneuvers.

The art of the white crane is generally considered a long-range fighting style, with many weapon sections involved. There are 14 basic hand and 10 weapon sets, which include the Buddha's disciple hand set (*lo han shou*). At the advanced stages of training students learn an internal pattern known as the cotton needle set. In ancient times the traditional method of practicing this set was on the *mui fa joong* (plum blossom poles). The method entailed burying the ends of 14 ten-foot poles into the ground to a depth of about three feet. These poles, placed two feet apart, were six inches in diameter, in a design which represented plum blossom (mui fa). Students would then perch themselves precariously on the top and begin to practice their forms. The sensation of height was intended to improve their balance and footwork. In some Chinese schools, sharpened bamboo stakes were placed in the ground beneath the poles, as a true test of courage. Today this practice is no longer in use. The modern version involves painting a mui fa upon the floor of the kwoon..

As we have seen, many styles and varieties of kung fu exist in China, the most popular of which we have already discussed. However, this is merely the tip of the iceberg for virtually every village in China at one time had a resident kung fu master. It is possible that styles exist today that no Westerner has ever seen. Even so, the fighting arts that this great country has given to the world, is the legacy handed down from the ancient masters in the hope that people will come to understand that the martial arts are not merely fighting techniques but also a pattern for living, which ultimately guide further, into the realms of beginning to understand oneself from within.

KARATE: THE ART OF THE EMPTY HAND

It is better to light a candle than to curse the dark

A goju ryu style take-down technique. A punch incorporates an arm and shoulder lock followed by a hammer fist, or tetsui, to the floating ribs. Two other possible target areas for the strike are the solar plexus and the face.

The trading routes of the Far East have been in existence for centuries and have been used by sailors, merchants and holy men to spread ideas, political ideologies, religion and news. So it would seem only natural that the island of Okinawa (the largest of the Ryukyu chain, strategically well-placed in the East China Sea) was the melting pot where many cultures merged. Okinawa was both a stepping-off point for many Pacific traders, and the birthplace of karate (not Japan, as many people believe).

The influence of the Chinese martial arts had reached Okinawa by the eleventh century, via Buddhist monks who had found their way to this island kingdom. Although the native Okinawans were a peace-loving people, possessing few combat techniques, they were intrigued by the simple kung fu methods of their Chinese visitors, and eagerly sought instruction.

Over the centuries they merged their fighting ability with that of the other Asian nations to produce an unarmed fighting system which they termed *te* or hand (though the more common native term used was *tode*). To distinguish this form of fighting from the Chinese boxing systems, foreigners called it *Okinawan te*.

Originally Okinawa was divided into three kingdoms, but was united in the fifteenth century by King Shohashi. In 1470 an edict was issued banning the possession of weapons to prevent would-be insurgents from building up armies to overthrow the king. One hundred and fifty years later, Okinawa's peaceful existence was rudely interrupted when, in 1609, the rulers of the Satsuma dynasty, the Shimazu clan, invaded Okinawa intent on turning it into a Japanese colony. Because of the ban on arms, the invading Japanese had little trouble in overcoming the Okinawan islanders who were quickly subdued. The occupying forces took the arms ban one step further and instituted a ban on any farming implement with a blade. Since all bladed tools were now locked up in a central warehouse, the farmers had to borrow their own tools off the Japanese for each day's work before returning them at dusk. This final restriction left the native islanders literally empty handed.

The word *karate* now means empty hand. (In 17th-century Okinawa the character for *kara* meant China and *te* meant hand.) The correct rendering for the name of the art is karate-do,

the word do means way. But in the 1930s the meaning of kara was changed to empty.

On Okinawa there was a settlement for the visiting Chinese missionaries and trade delegations, known as the nine villages, where 36 Chinese families set up home. Okinawa rebel leaders, opposed to the Japanese occupation, visited this area which was called Kumemura, to persuade the Chinese monks to teach them the empty-hand methods of Chinese boxing. Over the next 100 years the Okinawans blended the Chinese methods with their own ideas and eventually developed an indigenous fighting system. Three main schools of fighting emerged, known as *tomari-te, naha-te,* and *shuri-te*, each name deriving from the town where it developed. Most karate students in those days had to practice in secret lest their Japanese overlords discover and punish them with instant execution.

The sole reason why the Okinawas studied karate was to enable them to kill the Japanese invaders with one blow of their hands or feet. The Okinawans therefore pounded their knuckles and fingertips on hard surfaces to build up callouses as hard as iron. The rebel

一禮節を守り

一信義を重じ

一情實に瀰れず

一眞劍味を徹せよ

Left: *Chris Rowen, a goju ryu karate stylist, executing the traditional knife-hand block. Karateka of this style use a mixture of hard and soft techniques. The style is most predominant on the island of Okinawa.*

Above: *Two wado ryu stylists free sparring. A roundhouse kick is intercepted by a flying sidekick. Note that the attacker in the air has his foot guarding his groin.*

army did not need swords and spears, their hands and feet were just as effective. So, while they went into battle empty handed, they still defeated the heavily armed Japanese samurai time after time, using karate. Legends and folk tales grew up around these great heroes and stories circulated of how a master of Okinawa-te went into the forest to pick out a tree. He then pounded that tree every day with his hands and feet, punching the trunk thousands of times until it died. Then he knew he was ready to face the occupying forces. One story tells how a certain master of Naha-te could punch the ground with his fist with such power that his arm was buried up to his elbow.

It says much for the effectiveness of karate and the valor of the Okinawans that a simple peasant farmer armed with only his bare hands could defeat a skilled, well-trained and heavily armed samurai warrior. In those days the Japanese wore a type of lacquered bamboo armor which the Okinawans, with their hardened fingertips and using a technique called *spear hand* could pierce with a single blow. The spear hand also pierced the samurai's heart, killing him instantly. Another technique favored by the rebels was that of the flying side kick. When a rebel was suddenly confronted by a mounted samurai he would launch himself into the air using a kind of springing jump, then lash out his leg, striking the chest of the samurai with his rock-hard heel. The samurai went flying, falling to the ground probably with a smashed rib cage.

Above: *A young karateka of the kyokushinkai style demonstrates the use of the rice flail or nunchaku.*
Above right: *The nunchaku is a difficult weapon to master; it takes years of training to become skilled in its use.*
Right: *The traditional Okinawan sai being used to defend against an attack with a samurai sword. The sword is trapped in the sai's hilt and rendered useless. The defender then strikes with his second sai. This weapon is always used in pairs.*
Left: *A practitioner uses sais to block a lunge punch and attack the floating ribs, and simultaneously delivers a stamping kick to the knee joint.*

Left: *The karate lunge punch is capable of generating great power in its application. The screwing of the fist upon impact of a target can quite literally lift a full-grown man off his feet. Here Denise Rossell Jones, a 4th dan black belt, applies a punch that can nearly cut a man in two.*

Below: *Goju karate master, 5th dan James Rousseau, goes into the defense against a knife-hand strike to the eyes. The fist that is held at his side will be released to create the maximum amount of damage to his opponent.*

For all their valor and constant harassing of the enemy, the Okinawans had to resign themselves to the fact that the Japanese were there to stay. Eventually Okinawa merged with Japan both politically and culturally, and the Japanese, being a warrior race themselves, investigated this instant unarmed method of killing. Three hundred years later karate lives on, being practiced openly in Okinawa. There are now many different styles, and the art is even taught in schools.

In the early days of the formalized systems, each master developed his own special style. Although the techniques were very limited, sometimes to just one or two, some masters specialized in the one-punch blow, others in the elbow-strike maneuvers. A decade or so later, karate techniques began to adopt more of a systematic approach, and eventually various methods of blocking, kicking and striking were developed.

The greatest advance that karate made was when the new modernized Japanese navy sailed into Chujo Bay, Okinawa. The Imperial Japanese Fleet under Admiral Dewa was invited to a huge banquet. During this feast various demonstrations were arranged for the visitors, one being performed by a mild-mannered school teacher, Gichin Funakoshi, who revealed his own karate approach. Admiral Dewa was so impressed that, on his return to Japan, he told the emperor about this unarmed combat. The emperor invited Funakoshi to Kyoto to give a private demonstration of karate and this was how, in 1917, Okinawan-te was introduced to the country. However, it was not until 1 April 1922, when Funakoshi gave a formal demonstration of his karate at a girls' school in Tokyo, that the art of the empty hand was seen by the Japanese public.

Funakoshi was born in Shuri, Okinawa, in 1868, the son of a government official. He was a premature baby and a sickly child, often suffering from bouts of ill health. While attending primary school he made friends with a boy who was the son of the great karate master Yasutune Azato. Watching his young friend imitating his father's martial arts' movements was Funakoshi's first introduction to karate. By the time he was 13 years old his health had greatly improved and he was accepted as a student by Azato and his formal training in karate blossomed. Within 10 years he became something of an expert himself, training every free moment he could find.

As a school teacher, Funakoshi was in a good position to persuade the Okinawa Government that karate was an excellent means of promoting good health and discipline, both mental and physical. It was later introduced into the educational curriculum.

In 1922, after Funakoshi's public demonstration of karate, he was persuaded by Jigoro Kano (the founder of *judo*), to stay in Japan for a time and give more demonstrations of his art. It was through Kano's introductions into Japanese martial arts circles that Funakoshi and his karate became very popular. Aided by the press of the day, karate became known as the art that could kill a man with one blow and crush his internal organs without marking his skin. This sensational approach, although not wholly true, did much to spread the name of karate (which at that time was still known as Okinawan-te) throughout Japan. Nonetheless, the media's attitude upset Funakoshi because he had always been keen to emphasize the fact that karate was essentially for self-defense.

When Funakoshi was nearing his sixtieth birthday, an age when many people would be thinking of retirement, he opened up his first training school under the auspices of the great *kendo* teacher Nakayama. Funakoshi operated from a room in Nakayama's *dojo* (training hall) and called his school Shoto-Kan, the club of Shoto (Shoto had been Funakoshi's pen name when he used to write poetry, and means waving pines). Funakoshi used the school to lay down the foundations for the style of shotokan karate, the most popular style of karate in the world today.

Although Funakoshi's style had originally been based on Shuri-te, once in Japan he introduced new impetus into the art, drawing on his experiences with the other Okinawan masters with whom he had trained. He began to make subtle changes to the original style and modified it. In later years his son Yoshitaka became a driving force behind his style, creating the now famous *mawashigeri* or roundhouse kick and slowly changed it from its distinctive original form.

In the years following Funakoshi's arrival in Japan several other styles developed, some being introduced by Okinawan masters following in his footsteps. Each style had its own techniques and myriad fighting methods. Karate became so popular that, by the 1930s, all the major Japanese universities had thriving clubs and intense rivalries grew among the

Above: *One of the most difficult kicks in karate is the flying sidekick. The practitioner has to launch himself into the air from a near standing position, yet height has to be reached in order to gain the maximum advantage.*
Left: *Wado ryu instructor Chris Thompson traps his opponent's arm and delivers an empi or elbow strike. In karate all parts of the body become major weapons.*
Far left: *A roundhouse kick is delivered to the opponent's head area. This is known as a jodan or high-range kick.*

students of the different styles. Inevitably, due to the proliferation of styles, karate began to fragment. Adepts who had once been students were now instructors in their own right, developing their own styles.

At the outbreak of World War II the unarmed combat karate methods were taught to the troops of the Imperial Japanese Army but, when the Americans occupied Japan in 1945, the supreme commander of the allied forces, General Douglas MacArthur, placed a ban on all martial arts training. During the American occupation Yoshitaka Funakoshi, being fiercely nationalistic, refused American rations and consequently died of starvation. Martial arts historians later described Yoshitaka as the greatest genius in the history of karate.

With a return to peace after the war karate began to be organized on a worldwide level. In 1948 a karate demonstration was given at a US airbase. The Westerners were so impressed with what they saw that, two years later, the American Strategic Air Command (SAC) had more than 24 physical training instructors instructed in martial arts. By the mid-1950s Funakoshi himself had toured US airbases throughout the Far East, giving karate demonstrations to thousands of American airmen. It was mainly due to this series of exhibitions that the art of the empty hand was introduced to the West. And in 1953 karate was officially introduced to the United States: karate had finally come of age.

Two years after this red-letter day the Japanese Karate Association was formed, the largest governing body for one style in the world, with nearly six million practitioners. Gichin Funakoshi, who has been called the Father of Karate, died in April 1957 aged 88 years old. He had practiced his beloved art right up until his death.

Karate spread into Europe in the late 1950s through the efforts of French karate enthusiast Henri Plee. A student of Plee named Vernon Bell then brought karate to Britain. Today, every country in the world has at least one Japanese graded karate instructor. It took the better part of two thousand years for the martial arts to evolve and develop, and just 60 years for it to conquer the entire world.

All today's styles of karate stem from Okinawa and while they might initially look reasonably similar, are all subtly different. Modern karate is based almost entirely on

strikes and blocks, using high-impact kicks and punches. Depending upon the style practiced, the techniques are applied in various ways. Some styles prefer to block a punch using an open-palm hand, while others maintain that the fist should be clenched, lest the fingers are caught and bent back. It can be safely stated that there is no best style. Each one provides the student with a framework of training upon which to build and further his or her knowledge of technique application. It is up to each individual student to carry his or her potential to its maximum limit until eventually there is no limit at all. At this stage the student has risen beyond technique and into the spiritual bounds of mental development. This is the ultimate goal to which Funakoshi hoped all students would eventually aspire.

Shotokan karate is the style that Gichin Funakoshi formulated from early Okinawan styles. It is characterized by deep stances and powerful extended movements. The style has many *kata* (forms) which are practiced with

Above left: *The great karate sensei and founder of the shotokan karate style, master Gichin Funakoshi. He was responsible for introducing karate to Japan.*

Above: *The top Japanese master in England, sensei Enoeda demonstrating part of a kata.*
Right: *The founder of wado ryu karate, Master Otsuka (right), watches a knife-defense situation.*

emphasis on strength. The practice of kata was regarded by Funakoshi as 'the ultimate expression of his art.' With its most linear application the style uses considerable muscle power in its delivery. Beginners start by training in simple katas known as *heian katas* (heian means peaceful). There are five of these katas which originally were called *pinan*. These katas were created by one of Funakoshi's early teachers named Itosu for use in physical education classes in schools on Okinawa. Once the heian katas are mastered a whole plethora of katas are then introduced, each varying in degrees of difficulty and expertise.

Far left: *8th dan master Tatsuo Suzuki, a wado ryu stylist of extraordinary talent.*
Left: *Master Otsuka, the founder of wado ryu karate, just weeks before his death.*
Right: *Master Harunda Hoshino training in kata in the solitude of the hills.*
Below right: *Kanazawa sensei kneeling in the traditional seiza posture.*

One of the greatest students in the style today is Hirokazu Kanazawa, the famous competition fighter. In the first All-Japan Karate championships held in Tokyo in 1957 he won the free-fighting category *(kumite)* despite a broken hand. The following year he won the championships again, only this time he also took first place in the kata section as well. In later years, in an effort to improve his understanding and extend his knowledge of martial arts, he began a serious study and practice of the internal Chinese art tai chi chuan.

Wado ryu karate (way of peace), was created by one of Funakoshi's senior students named Hidenori Otsuka. Otsuka's training in martial arts began in his childhood. He was born in 1892 and spent much of his youth studying *shindo yoshin ryu jujitsu*. Otsuka, after many years of study, gained the headmastership of the style. He was first introduced to karate through judo inventor Dr Kano. He immediately began to train in the art, although he was by then over 30 years old. After spending more than 10 years with Funakoshi he broke away from shotokan to formulate his own style. For a time Otsuka's karate had no proper name, but in 1940 at a huge martial arts festival he was asked to register the name of his school, and called it wado ryu (ryu means school).

As Otsuka began to make distinct changes in his karate, he drew heavily upon his knowledge of jujitsu, which he merged with the shotokan techniques. This resulted in more upright stances and more fluid techniques than in shotokan. This amalgamation of the yielding principles of jujitsu, with its emphasis of non-opposition to strength, and the traditional Okinawan karate maneuvers gave a softness to wado ryu unique in Japanese karate.

Otsuka's wado ryu is a tremendously fast style. Its techniques and movements are the total expression of the practitioner's mind as manifested in his spirit. Otsuka always emphasized that the *karateka* (one who practices karate) should always hold true three vital elements – the heart, spirit and physical strength. Otsuka is also remembered because he formulated the first principles of *kumite* (the free sparring in karate) which was the forerunner of sport or competition karate as we now know it. It is the sparring element in today's karate that prompts advocates to learn the art. It seems strange that karate caught on with such tremendous fervor in Japan, solely as a way of practicing kata.

Otsuka's unrelenting services to karate were rewarded when the Emperor of Japan's brother awarded him his tenth dan black belt. And shortly before his death on 29 January 1982, just four months short of his ninetieth birthday, Otsuka was recognized as the oldest practicing karateka in the world. Since his death the wado style has spread all over the world. Interestingly, in the eight bi-annual world championships so far held, in which over 50 nations compete, one team has won four times. The consistently successful team is from Great Britain, with two-thirds of its members being wado stylists.

Because wado ryu employs very light and fast techniques, the style favors evasion, not the head-on clash of brute force. After delivering a technique, the hand or foot is snapped back very quickly to avoid being captured by the opponent. Students are taught to punch by creating a very fast type of whiplash movement involving a certain amount of hip twisting to increase the force of the punch.

Kyokushinkai karate was the brainchild of the Korean martial artist Masatatsu Oyama, who was also a student of shotokan under Funakoshi. The name, meaning style of the ultimate truth, was arrived at when Oyama left Funakoshi to retire to the mountains of Chiba in Japan to meditate and search for a deeper meaning to the empty-hand art. Oyama had been greatly influenced by the Chinese and Korean martial arts but he was not too impressed with shotokan as a fighting technique. During his two-year period of self-inflicted isolation he learned how to become one with his environment and, through deep meditative procedures and intensive training, formulated an entirely new system of karate based exclusively on combat effectiveness. He named this new style *kyokushinkai*.

When Oyama returned to civilization he created a certain amount of media interest when he announced that he could kill a full-grown bull with his bare hands. Furthermore, he invited the press to a local slaughterhouse where he fought a short-horned bull, eventually killing the beast with a knife-hand strike to the head. On another occasion when he was fighting a bull, he used the karate chop and sliced its horn in half. During his bullfighting period, Oyama fought 50 bulls, killing three of them outright with striking techniques.

Oyama has never struck rigidly to the traditional techniques of karate, and has looked beyond the art for more effective methods of self-defense to incorporate into his own system. In the early 1970s Oyama introduced a new competition onto the tournament scene which he termed *knockdown*. This form of fighting allows full-power strikes to the body and kicks to the head. The bout ends when one of the two competitors is knocked to the ground. This, Oyama stated, 'is the only true test of a karateka's fighting ability.' The training in kyokushinkai style is very severe, and is probably the toughest of all the karate systems. But despite its tough training, kyokushinkai still employs the traditional training of kata.

Kenwa Mabuni, a contemporary of Gichin Funakoshi, also studied under one of his masters, Itosu. Mabuni created the karate style known as *shito ryu* (the name is derived from Mabuni's two instructors, Itosu and Higaonna and the word shito comes from the Japanese characters used to write his teachers' names).

With the popularity of karate in Japan in the early 1920s, other Okinawan teachers were summoned to teach the art. Kenwa Mabuni followed in Funakoshi's footsteps and went to Japan to teach the art, opening his first club in Osaka in 1934. His main vehicle for teaching karate was the traditional method of kata, Mabuni's penchant for kata led him to assimilate as many different styles as possible, and he was influenced by shotokan, *goju ryu*, and many of the early shorin katas, leading to over 60 katas (including those involving weapons) for this one system.

In the same way that many of Funakoshi's senior students left him to form their own styles, so too did Mabuni's. One of the more famous was Chojiro Tani, who broke away to develop his own theories on karate aimed at the increasingly popular tournament circuit. Tani named his hybrid style *shukokai.*

Above: *Masatatsu Oyama, the founder of kyokushinkai karate.*

Above right: *A trio of blackbelt triplets perform kata in unison.*

Freely translated shukokai means way for all. Tani's modern version of the shito style could not have a more appropriate name, for it has been adopted by many of the world's leading competition fighters, and is a proven tournament winner. Through experimentation and research, Tani developed a higher fighting stance, similar to that of wado ryu. He instigated faster kicks and direct-blocking methods which were implemented with open-hand palm blocks rather than clenched, tight-fist blocks, as found in many other styles. Tani felt that to win a competition the fighter had to be extremely fast and mobile, with the delivery of the attack being more important than anything else. The shorter, more upright stance, unlike the low, wide stance of styles like shotokan, led to increased speed and helped to promote good mobility.

The style teaches its students to relax before the impact of a punch, thereby increasing acceleration and creating a greater force. Tani introduced into the training sessions foam punchpads, held by one student and hit by another, who can feel the power he has generated in this particular technique. This innovation completely revolutionized the old system in which students spent weeks just punching thin air. The kicking techniques of

Tani's style were further enhanced with the introduction of combination techniques which swept aside the old theory that if it took more than one blow to down an opponent, the student was not putting everything into his first punch.

The basic stance of the style is a natural one, of a person simply walking. The system also emphasizes open-hand techniques to avoid muscle tension, believing that if a student clenches the fist he will instinctively tighten the muscles. In contrast, the open hand allows a flexible wrist action which allows a faster punching or blocking action. However, one of Tani's leading students, Yoshinao Nanbu, became disillusioned with shukokai even though he had carved a name for himself as a successful tournament fighter. Nanbu had won the All-Japan Students Karate Championships three times but, with his sights set upon becoming a leading master, he left the style that had brought him fame to drift into other systems to see what they had to offer.

For about three years Nanbu apparently disappeared, before reappearing with a style that he named *sankukai*. Although it was not one of the most popular styles in the karate world it did attract a certain following, and bore a remarkable resemblance to some Chinese systems (though it was predominantly Japanese) prompting some martial artists to think that Nanbu must have travelled to the Chinese mainland during his three-year disappearance. Sankukai stylists began to make some headway in tournaments, when Nanbu suddenly left his own organization. Once again he re-emerged some years later with yet another style of karate, only this time it had more of a Chinese flavor, and owed little to his Japanese background. He named this style after himself, *Nanbudo* or the way of Nanbu. The style places great stress upon a health exercise known as *Nanbu taiso* which is similar to tai chi but involves jerky rather than flowing movements.

Goju ryu karate was created by an Okinawan named Chojun Miyagi. Goju ryu karate means hard-soft style, and is based on the yin and yang principles of the soft and hard. It was developed from the art of naha-te. Miyagi began training in the naha-te system when he was little more than 14 years old under the great instructor Kanryo Higaonna. As a youth Higaonna had made many trips to China while working for an import and export company. During one of these trips he decided to stay on the Chinese mainland and, while there, became greatly interested in Chinese boxing. Upon his return some years later, he merged

visit to Shanghai on the Chinese mainland Chojun Miyagi had modified to a certain extent some of the finer points of Goju. However, Yamaguchi refused to accept these modifications, believing that the old ways were the best, and broke away from the goju movement and wandered up into the mountains.

Miyagi devoted his whole life to the teaching and furtherance of goju ryu karate, which has remained unchanged right up to the present day (unlike other styles which were splintering and becoming almost unrecognizable from the original forms). Miyagi died on 8 October 1953, aged 65.

The techniques in *goju kai* involve close-in fighting. This is a highly complex style that is quite exacting, requiring a balance between

Left: *Master Chojun Miyagi, the founder of Okinawan goju ryu.*
Below: *Master Gogen Yamaguchi, known affectionately as 'the cat,' the founder of goju kai in Japan.*
Below right: *Now a 10th dan master, Gogen Yamaguchi still practices his karate every day.*
Below, far right: *The son of Gogen Yamaguchi preparing to deliver a knife-hand strike. He is now a full-time karate teacher in San Francisco.*

his ideas of the Chinese systems with those of the indigenous karate systems of Okinawa. Although goju was developed from naha-te, its Chinese influence is easily recognizable.

Two of Higaonna's top students were Miyagi and Mabuni. After their master's death they took his place as the school's instructors, but Miyagi soon decided to travel to the Chinese mainland as his teacher had done before him. Continuing his studies in China, Miyagi was greatly influenced by the internal systems of *kung fu* and the special breathing techniques. He began to understand that karate, with the added impetus of kung fu, could be twice as deadly. Miyagi returned home to Okinawa some years later with a greater knowledge and understanding and quickly established himself as a karate teacher.

Following in Funakoshi's footsteps, Miyagi went to Japan where Okinawan instructors were in great demand to take up his position as karate teacher at Kyoto University. Although he was very successful, attracting large classes, he began to get so homesick that he returned to Okinawa. While some of his students followed him to Okinawa, one student, Gogen Yamaguchi, began to formulate his own karate techniques. This happened because during a

hard and soft. This balance gives the student the ability to change techniques in a quick flowing manner in order to execute a kick or punch with the force of a thunderbolt. The training methods of goju kai are not based upon muscular strength alone; a great deal of emphasis is placed upon special breathing techniques. A beginner must master these correctly in order to gain mastery of the complete system. Originally, goju had no high kicks whatsoever but modern sporting ideas have introduced a certain number of these into the style. Traditionally, high kicks to the head were not employed because they were considered unsafe, because the overextended line of balance was too exaggerated.

Goju kai karate came into being through the developments made from the original form of goju ryu by Yamaguchi. While in the mountains seeking spiritual guidance, after he had left Miyagi's goju ryu, he became invovled with a group of Shinto priests. Under their tutorship Yamaguchi followed the path of nature. He began a hard training regimen involving deep meditational practices, and went without food or drink for long periods of time. Every morning he would stand in the traditional goju stance of *sanchin* (hourglass stance) under the icy waters of a mountain waterfall. His strength and mental abilities increased tremendously during his mountain period. When Yamaguchi returned to civilization his style of goju kai soon became very important in Japanese martial circles. His goju kai spread, becoming far more popular than his master's system of goju ryu.

Throughout the late 1930s, as goju kai became increasingly popular, its grandmaster Yamaguchi became affectionately known as 'the cat.' At the outbreak of World War II when Yamaguchi was serving in the forces he was captured by the Russians and shipped off to a labor camp in Mongolia. Yamaguchi's indomitable karate spirit kept him alive through this wretched period, when many around him were dying. At the end of the war, after more than 12 months in captivity, he was repatriated and returned home to Japan. In 1948 he opened his new karate *dojo* (club) and began establishing goju kai all over again. In 1950 he formed the All-Japan Karate-do Goju-kai and later was awarded the tenth dan black belt.

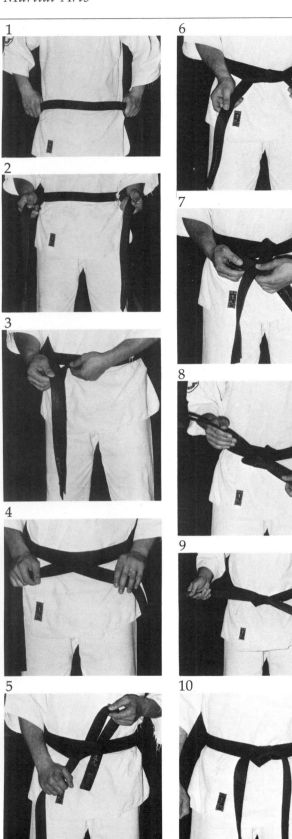

Yamaguchi is still greatly respected and is one of the few living great masters of karate. His devotion to karate can be gauged from his reply to a student's question, 'What is karate all about?' His answer, which perhaps sums up the essence of goju kai, was 'karate is not about fighting; it is about truth. The karate I teach cannot be understood without exploring and studying some aspects of the shinto religion and yoga, and then applying this knowledge to the art of karate itself.'

Discipline in goju kai clubs is very strict, as it is in all the Japanese karate styles (this is not the case in the West). For example, in a goju kai club everyone scrubs the floors on their hands and knees, and cleans out the toilets. This happens everyday and absolutely no one, no matter what rank they hold, is excluded from this task.

Training in karate varies greatly from club to club, depending upon what style the novice adopts and also which country he is living in. For instance, in the Eastern countries discipline is far more severe and techniques are learned slowly and thoroughly. In the West, however, although discipline is strict it is not enforced as strictly as in the East and teaching methods are not so detailed. Consequently, students can expect to gain a black belt far more quickly than a contemporary in the East. The other essential difference between West and East is that we regard the black belt as an expert who has finished his training, whereas Easterners regard the black belt as being at the beginning of all true karate training.

The colored belt system was invented by the Japanese. A beginner starts off with a light colored belt and, as he progresses, dyes his belt, gradually making it darker until it is finally black. The belt system does a number of things: it immediately signals a student's standing in the karate syllabus; it gives him something to aim for; and finally it satisfies the ego. Each karate association or style has its own colored belt grading system. Consequently if two students, each learning a different martial art, wear the green belt this does not mean that they have reached the same standard.

1. Place the middle of the belt against your suit. 2. Wrap the belt around your waist, crossing one side over the other as they meet behind you. 3. Bring the ends forward and around your waist again. 4. Pass the left hand end under the right hand end, and cross it at the front. 5. Push the right-hand end under both layers of the belt and (6) pull it over and out. 7. Pass the right hand end over the top of the left hand end and (8) push or thread under and out of the top of the loop. 9. Pull both ends tight. 10. The completed knot.

Right: *Paul Coleman demonstrates a goju ryu take-down technique. The student is finished off with a punch to his nose.*

Left: *This Great Britain team has won the WUKO world karate championships on no less than four separate occasions. Even the Japanese hold these fighters in awe. They were led to victory by their team manager David 'Ticky' Donovan.*
Right: *Shotokan students on a training seminar.*
Below right: *Shotokan instructor sensei Kawazoa shows a student how to apply the shuto, or knife-hand strike correctly.*

In the early days of Okinawan karate, grades were not deemed necessary because in the eyes of the masters you either succeeded or failed – there was no in between. And even when karate arrived in Japan there were only two belts, the white (which denoted the novice) and the black (indicating a higher level of proficiency). It was only when the West became interested in karate that the many colors were introduced as a way of rewarding achievement.

The colored belt stage is known as *kyu* and there are nine in most styles. Beginners start at grade nine, receiving one particular colored-belt and, as they progress, so they either receive a different colored belt or a different colored tag to sew on to the belt ending. Absolute beginners usually wear a white belt and, within the first six to eight weeks, take a grading test. Very few, if any, fail this exam which demands competence in the basic stance, in executing a kick and a punch, plus a few other basic techniques. The reason it is rare for anyone to fail this first grading is that they will be all the keener to progress and also feel that they belong to the karate world.

Grading tests usually take place every three months and, providing the student is success-ful, he will eventually tackle a kata. A kata is a set pattern of movements in which the practi-tioner defends himself or herself against a series of imaginary opponents. The aim is to develop timing, balance and focus. At first the student learns simple katas, gradually master-ing the lengthier and more difficult ones. Al-though the different styles have different names for their katas, they are all basically the same. By the time the student reaches the fourth kyu he will have his sights firmly set upon the next grade, which in most styles is the first brown belt. Since at this point flawless techniques are expected, the student must spend more time mastering his art, and con-sequently the advanced student can only take two grading exams a year.

Eventually the time comes when the student is a first kyu. The next test, which will be the hardest to date, is the test for black belt or *shodan* (sho means first, dan means degree or class). A dan grade is allowed to wear a black belt. The time required to reach shodan stage is from three to five years, depending upon the style practiced and the student's ability.

The successful student becomes a black belt 1st dan. A common fallacy is that once a student reaches black belt life becomes a little easier. But training does not cease, in fact it becomes even more arduous for the black belt must now train in the mental aspects of karate as well as the physical. After a year or so the shodan can go in for his next examination which is for *nidan* or second-degree black belt (this does not mean that if he passes the test he can wear two black belts). Since the term ni denotes second, the wearer usually adds a small tag or stripe to the end of his black belt.

After a certain amount of time, again depending upon which style of karate is being studied, the third or fourth dan black belt stops taking grading examinations. From now on all dan grades are awarded either by the relevant association or the world head of that particular style. Grades are bestowed for many reasons, such as time spent mastering karate, services to the art, or gaining great distinction in tournaments. For instance in 1984 David 'Ticky' Donovan, the Great Britain team manager and coach, was awarded the rank of seventh dan for his services to karate and his coaching ability by the World Union of Karate Organizations.

It is interesting to note that after the grade of eighth dan (in some styles ninth dan) the black belt reverts to red, which is the traditional color of a beginner's belt, before he takes his first kyu test. This symbolizes the fact that when a martial artist knows all he must return to the source knowing nothing, yet understanding everything.

The karate training hall is a *dojo* and does not necessarily have to be indoors. A dojo can be a disused factory room, a garage or even a basement. The karate student is a karateka and his suit or uniform is termed a *karate-gi*. Some teachers are sticklers for etiquette, inculcating in the student a respect for his art and his fellow students. So, for instance, before beginning any technique, the practitioner must bow to his or her opponent. Also, each training session begins and ends with all the students lining up

Above, all three: *Goju practitioner Master Higaonna training with iron weights to promote strength and power.*
Below right: *A student practices his kata in the relative quiet of his dojo.*

Below: *A karateka adopts the pose of the horse stance. This classic stance is seen in martial arts all over the world. It strengthens the legs.*

Below right: *A karateka executes a block.*
Below, far right: *This block and punch is strong.*

Above right: *A young woman competitor executes her kata during a competition kata section.*
Above far right: *In kata competition, points are scored for the most flawless execution.*

Left: *Japan takes first and second place in the kata section in the 1984 world championships. Seen here with the gold medal is Sakamoto, who has won this slot three times in succession. Japan's rigid attention to detail within the kata form ensures gold medals every time.*
Below: *Goju karate practitioners demonstrate the use of power-training implements at a tournament.*

and then stooping to their knees to bow to their *sensei* (teacher or instructor) as a mark of respect.

All karate styles are based on a certain number of basic techniques. The single moves are then joined together to create what are termed *combination techniques* which consist of a step, followed by a punch and a kick. To perfect these techniques to any standard of competency long hours of muscle-straining repetitions are required, as each technique is practiced over and over again until it is indelibly inscribed upon the student's brain. Such training methods ensure that when a student is attacked he will automatically retaliate with the correct move. All karate systems work on the premise of reflex action thus cutting out or eliminating the thinking process. When the mind and body become one, they react as one thus facilitating the tremendous speeds that a karateka can generate in both defense and attack. Repetition results in perfect technique.

Since these basics take much time to learn, students should not try to take short cuts, thus defeating the object of the spiritual and inner learning process. If a student simply picks and chooses the most accessible features from a certain style, ignoring the time-honored building blocks, then he will not realize his full potential as a martial artist and will, in all probability, fail.

In every traditional karate style there is a device for teaching timing, focus, balance, and co-ordination. It is called kata but is also known as patterns, or forms. Basically kata is an established series of movements in which the martial artist defends himself or herself against a series of imaginary attacks from one or more opponents. Kata is performed as a solo exercise in order for the student to gain mastery over techniques with or without an instructor being present, thus enabling students to practice at home as often as liked.

The old Okinawan masters believed that the secret of karate lay within the confines of the kata. In all modern-day tournaments and competitions the kata section attracts the largest number of entrants. Competition kata is judged upon how well each individual performs the sequential movements of a particular kata, laying special emphasis on sharp techniques, correct breathing, and the correct order and understanding of the movements. To the onlooker kata resembles a strange kind of dance. An expert will build up as much explosiveness and speed as possible and will completely lose himself or herself in the movement. Kata provides the opportunity for the adept to execute a vast range of techniques that are forbidden in competition fighting. Many karate exponents spend their whole lives just perfecting the movements and mental awareness needed in kata. The great master Gichin Funakoshi believed that from kata every technique in karate can be learned.

Kata can be practiced blindfolded, thus developing positional sense, and in fact almost a sixth sense concerning one's own and other movements in the immediate vicinity. The various styles of karate place a different emphasis on kata, some schools have more than 60 different ones in their curriculum, whereas others have as few as 15.

Karate practice requires a high degree of physical fitness. Therefore, before a typical karate class commences with techniques training, the whole assembly undergoes a series of physical training exercises that are aimed at improving stamina, muscle development, and flexibility through leg stretching procedures. With the introduction of sports karate karateka found that they required a higher degree of physical stamina. With this in mind and the introduction of sports medicine in the early 1970s, karate enthusiasts adopted a new area for stamina training based upon the scientific principles of the functioning of the human body. Consequently, top karate fighters of international and world standard tuned their bodies to afford them the maximum physical and mental performances in the sports arena.

During a typical competition the actual sparring consists of a free exchange of blows, blocks and counterattacks until one of the fighters (more correctly termed players) gets a fully focused blow to the target area. In real terms the blow falls a fraction of an inch short of actually hitting the opponent. The referee determines if the strike was either delivered with meaning and focus, or if it was well timed and aimed at the appropriate area, in which case a point is awarded. The term *ippon* is a full point, which is awarded for a particularly good technique. A *wazari* is a half point awarded when the technique is good but not perfect. At the end of a specified time the points are counted up to find the winner.

The only really standardized scoring approach has been adopted by the governing

Above: *The United States versus Germany in the 1985 semi-contact karate tournament.*

Above, far left: *Ed Parker, the founder of American kempo, and the man who introduced Bruce Lee to the American tournament circuit scene.*

Above left: *Benny 'the jet' Urquidez, one of America's greatest kickboxers. He held three separate world kickboxing titles at once.*

Far left: *Two kickboxers practicing their techniques. Fighters need to develop very supple legs in order to execute very high kicks.*

Left: *George Bruckner of Berlin, West Germany. Credited as the father of European full-contact karate, he is now European president of WAKO.*

Right: *Fighters kitted out in standard safety equipment.*

Left: *Two shotokan stylists fighting in competition at world level. This IAKF competition held in Japan is an alternative organization to WUKO.*

Right: *Women's kumite, or free fighting, has caught on in a big way in recent years. Here Britain's Janice Argyle delivers a roundhouse kick to her German opponent during the 1984 world championships.*

Below right: *A superb roundhouse kick stops a competitor in his tracks.*

Below: *At major karate tournaments it is not unusual to see more than one fight going on at a time. Quite often four areas are needed for the elimination bouts.*

body for karate, the World Union of Karate Organizations (WUKO) which has more than 50 member countries under its banner. WUKO has held a world karate tournament every two years, since 1976. Great Britain has won the world team championships on four occasions. Although the standard of fighting seems to suit the Western practitioners of karate, it is interesting to note that what Funakoshi regarded as the ultimate in karate, the kata, has been won at every WUKO tournament (in both the women's and men's sections) by the Japanese.

It was inevitable that even on the traditional tournament scene karate would splinter and develop different styles. Karate tournaments were often too difficult for non-practitioners to follow, the rules were not clear, and the means of finding a winner was a complete mystery. To overcome such problems the martial arts factions in the United States devised a system known as full-contact karate which differed from the traditional form of the art where body contact was forbidden. In the new system, participants wear Western-style boxing gloves and fight in an ordinary boxing ring, while using the punching and kicking techniques of karate. And, as the name denotes, contestants can actually hit each other.

The idea quickly caught on and attracted a huge following, particularly when contests were screened at peak television time. Meanwhile, the Professional Karate Association (PKA) was established to guarantee a steady stream of competent fighters, many of whom became household names not just across the United States but throughout the world.

Full-contact karate soon spread from the United States to all corners of the world. Ironically, while the martial art of karate began in the East it was the Westerners who really popularized it as a sport. From full-contact karate came another split – semi-contact, which is much lighter in its application. Within a few years the semi-contact format had virtually replaced all traditional areas of karate competition in the United States. Semi-contact rules became known as the points system, which is today practiced more than any other kind of karate. In some contests novices wear special protective headgear and body armor which is cushioned with padding to prevent serious injury from kicks. Audiences love both full- and semi-contact matches, and even newcomers to the sport can quickly latch on to the rules. They have created such a demand for the sport that in the 1970s Hollywood made heroes out of karate fighters, who dominated the screen for the first time since Bruce Lee created a new icon in the 1960s.

Whenever one visits a training school for karateka, shouts or screams pierce the ear drums. These shouts are known as *kiais* (meaning spirit meeting). The kiai is a shout of power, similar to the war whoop of the Indian brave or the cry 'geronimo' when a paratrooper jumps from a plane. The kiai shout summons extra energy, a vital surge of adrenalin. This shout is usually made when performing a karate technique, and is executed at the moment of impact. The force behind this yell must be initiated from the very depths of the lower abdomen and, when performed with the correct control and timing, can stun an opponent. The masters of old were even said to have been able to knock a person out with a correct application of a kiai, while some Japanese experts could apparently kill a small bird with this spirit shout. All karateka learn this shout of power right at the start of their training. Even when practicing kata, kiais afford the practitioner the maximum power at vital points in the solo exercise.

The principle behind a kiai is firstly to

Left: *A gyaku tsuki or reverse punch, with the kiai or super-power shout. All styles of karate have this punch incorporated into their systems. It is probably the most powerful punching technique in karate.*

Above: *The US karate champion Mike Stone, was one of the greatest light-contact champions of the 1960s. In 1968 he came out of retirement and won the World Professional Light Heavyweight championship.*

create a surge of energy just at the right moment. Secondly, because the kiai occurs at the moment of exhalation, the diaphragm is empty of air and should an opponent strike at that very moment the defender is not caught with a lung full of air and consequently winded. The added bonus of emitting a kiai during a fight is that the unsuspecting assailant will probably be frightened by this sudden scream. It can make all the difference between winning and losing.

Until recent times women have only featured in karate competitions in the kata section. But constant demands by the women themselves led to the instigation of a free-fighting section for them in most major tournaments. Many joined the ranks of kickboxers, fighting in the rings of full-contact karate.

Right: *Women now take part in major full-contact kickboxing tournaments. Marguerite Hilliard (left) and Geraldine Leggett are both champions in their own right.*

Below: *The martial arts are a useful means of self-defense.*

Far right: *Two young women engage in semi-contact karate at tournament level.*

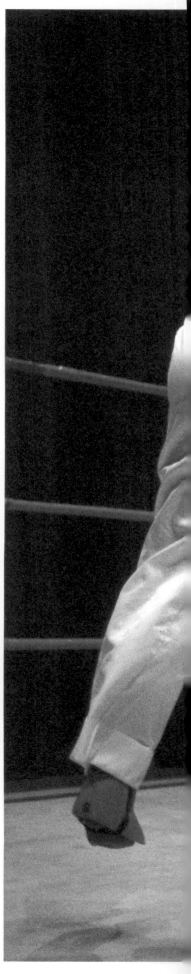

The most popular image of the karate expert is of someone smashing a stack of roofing tiles with one strike of his fist. This is called *tamashiwara*, or power breaking. Apart from being the exhibitionist side of the art, tamashiwara is also a constructive tool for improving one's karate.

When exponents concentrate their focused power upon one object, be it a block of wood or a roofing tile, they are actually testing themselves, measuring their ability and self-confidence. The mind must override the fact that skin and bone is being pitted against solid concrete, ensuring that the hand will not be smashed to pieces. Overcoming this fear factor is the vital ingredient of success.

A student can be called on to break many objects, ranging from a concrete slab to a block of ice, using a blow or strike from the head, hands, feet or elbow. When a karateka achieves his or her first successful break he or she becomes immediately aware of the tremendous power which has been harnessed.

In recent years new competitions have grown up for the power breakers, and adepts have created a forum for breaking materials of all shapes, sizes, and dimensions. In a tama-shiwara challenge the winner is the karateka who can break the greatest number of slabs with one strike. Kyokushinkai supremo Masa-tatsu Oyama still holds the record; he broke 30 roofing tiles with one blow. One of the most recent attempts at setting up a world record was in England when a power breaker named John Bowen smashed his way through a stack of solid granite chip kerbing stones with a single elbow smash.

Traditionally, some schools of karate advocated that students toughen up their knuckles on a device known as a *makiwara*. It is a striking post that is embedded a third of its length in the ground, the uppermost part being wrapped in layer after layer of straw. The karateka then pounds the post day after day in order to build large callouses on his fist.

On Okinawa the practice is still very much in fashion, although in the West this practice is no longer actively encouraged. Western doctors have found that with the constant use of a makiwara, the metacarpal bones in the hand became seriously impaired and disfigured, and in later life result in the severe arthritis.

The most vital ingredient of successful karate is the mind. And when the will and the body are harnessed as one unit, backed up with the finely honed skills of the ancient masters, success is guaranteed. The future of karate, however, is less certain, for at the moment the Eastern methods of training are in the process of evolution. Constant changes are being introduced by modern experts in an effort to bring karate into the twentieth century, and provide Japan with medals in the world's top tournaments. But with all this change, one wonders whether these time-tested arts are perhaps losing track of the true aims and principles of the way of the empty hand.

Above left: *Sensei John Bowen, the ex-world power-breaking champion, slams his elbow through ten granite-chip blocks.*
Left: *Solid pack-ice is just another material power breakers use when applying their technique. Here a karateka smashes three blocks of ice with a knife-hand strike.*
Above right: *A karate student practicing his punching on a makiwara. Constant use builds up callouses, producing a fist like iron.*
Right: *A goju karate master tensing his body to build up internal power.*

THE WARRIOR ARTS
OF JAPAN

*A man who has attained mastery o
an art reveals it in his every action*

The sand and rock garden
at Ryoanji Zen Temple in
Kyoto, Japan. Every day
the monks rake the sand
around the rocks so that
there is a constant number
of lines.

Because warfare has changed so dramatically within the last hundred years or so, individual skills on the battlefield are no longer necessary. Many of today's martial arts were once battlefield skills devised for the sole purpose of causing death or injury to an adversary. Now that modern concepts of warfare have introduced more sophisticated killing methods the ancient skills have been relegated to artistic disciplines. And many of these old martial arts have been developed to such an extent that, paradoxically, where they once were used to kill, they are now the means of self-development and personal enlightenment. Today's practitioners learn how fighting energy can be chanelled within to temper the spirit, and unite mind and body in peaceful harmony.

To the samurai of old, victory in combat was the absolute priority. His *katana* (sword) was his main weapon and was held with such high regard that it was known as the 'soul' of the warrior. The ancient samurai trained in the art of *kenjutsu*, or sword art, from which the practice of kendo developed. It has been said that the history of kendo is the history of the sumurai, the warrior class in feudal Japan.

Kendo developed from the battlefield art of kenjutsu (the sole aim of which was to kill an enemy) into a modern combat sport. Kendo (meaning way of the sword) is a disciplined sporting concept which still retains its respect for an opponent and the fighting spirit. It is essentially about probing beneath the surface, and journeying beyond technique. It is quite impossible to discuss kendo without touching on Zen which, as we have already seen, came to Japan from China. In Japan it took a dramatic turn and was adopted by the warrior class (samurai) who used it to increase self-reliance and to detach the self from emotional and material ends.

Zen gave the samurai the means to follow the concept of *mushin* (no mind). This enabled the samurai to empty his mind and become immune to outside disturbances. The term 'no mind' means that all trivia is rejected, leaving the mind naturally pliant and active, able to act or react without hindrance. To the swordsman, this state of mind could make all the difference between life and death. The no-mind state also establishes the concept of a spirit, rather like a sixth sense. Once a samurai had developed his inner self he was capable of swift, spontaneous actions in defending his own life, or as a matter of honor. Almost before an enemy had contemplated drawing his sword to kill the samurai, the warrior would have sensed the hostile action and taken instant steps to combat the threat. The Zen meditation techniques were also a means for preparing the samurai's mind for the exacting disciplines of military life in the feudal era.

As with most of the martial arts (or more correctly martial ways) in Japan today, kendo is regarded as a spiritual discipline. When two combatants face each other their aim is not to kill, but to strike and gain a point. This is achieved by observing and taking advantage of a weakness in an opponent's defense, created

Below: *The typical dress of a fully attired Samurai warrior. The armor is made of leather thongs and lacquered bamboo strips. Michael Jay is the only Western samurai.* **Above right:** *The first Japanese diplomatic delegation in Paris, 1862. Note that all the delegation are armed with twin swords, denoting that they are samurai.* **Below right:** *Samurai in full armor, bearing (left to right), the naginata, the yumi, and the yari.*

by an error of judgment. The weapon of the kendoka (one who practices kendo) is the *shinai*, or bamboo sword. This sword consists of four strips of bamboo held together at strategic points by cord.

Originally, samurai warriors were taught fencing with a live or real blade, and then at a later date used a training sword called a *bokken*. Usually made of heavy red oak, the bokken was the same shape, weight and balance of a real sword and could cause severe injuries and kill. Hence the introduction of the shinai. The use of the shinai meant that blows could be struck on the opponent's body rather than just on his sword or bokken. This allowed the student to try complex and multiple techniques time and time again, without the risk of the heavy bokken smashing in his opponent's head or body if he failed.

At the beginning of the Meiji restoration in 1868, an edict was issued banning the samurai from wearing swords in public. This edict was instrumental in making kendo more acceptable as a method of self-discipline, and also making the art rise to new heights of popularity. A little later the Japanese Minister of Education passed a regulation that made kendo compulsory in all schools. The character-building qualities of kendo was the main purpose for introducing the art to the classroom.

Below: *A watercolor of Tomoe, a mounted woman warrior from the Genji period in Japan.*
Above: *A watercolor shows the many stages of a samurai attiring himself in the complicated armor that he would wear on the battlefield. This procedure is seen today in many Japanese martial arts.*

Below: *A Japanese watercolor depicts a group of invading samurai being stopped at a bridge by retainers of a rival lord.*

Right: *A Japanese print by Kunisada depicts a samurai without armor. Even so, the samurai would never be seen without his twin swords.*

At the end of World War II the American occupying forces under General MacArthur banned the practice of all martial arts. But by 1951 the ban was lifted and kendo was re-introduced into secondary schools. At first Japan's postwar youth did not seem too interested in anything to do with militarism. But, gradually, kendo gained ground and eventually became as popular as ever. Active competition was encouraged and the sport soon attracted international interest and also led to the formation of a Japanese governing body. The members outlined a series of rules and regulations to standardize all tournaments throughout the world. In spite of this, however, kendo has changed so greatly, even in the last hundred years, that some martial artists feel that the original concept has now become diluted and ineffective.

A modern kendo enthusiast has to be fully protected before he fights. His costume consists of a light cotton blouse and an ankle-length split skirt known as a hakama. The protective armor is called *dogu* and consists of a *tare*, which is a waist and groin protector, while the *do* or breastplate is made from either fiber or bamboo and is covered in highly lacquered leather. A wide-fitting headband called a *hachimaki* is wrapped around the forehead to soak up the perspiration so that it does not run into the kendoka's eyes. The face-mask or *men* is constructed from steel and brass, with a protective grille running horizontally across the face. The final piece of equipment is the *kote*, a glove resembling a gauntlet which protects the hands from the shinai. A certain amount of traditional ritual is followed when the kendoka attires himself in his uniform prior to a kendo practice.

In competition kendo there are eight ways of scoring. Seven of them are with direct blows, and one with a thrust. The blows resemble blade-cutting motions – although in competition a shinai is used without the blade – and the

thrust is a lunge at the throat. Whereas in karate competitions the rules are often quite hard for the uninitiated to follow, and the scoring even harder, in kendo it is much simpler. When a scoring blow is struck, the part of the body that has been hit is called out, enabling the spectator to follow the match.

In kendo great emphasis is placed on the footwork, which is regarded as second in importance only to eyesight. After the student has learned the basic kendo sword strokes and stances, he or she advances on to *surburi* which is the co-ordination of arm and foot movements. The footwork steps must be carried out in unison with the arm movements. Kendo footwork involves stepping and sliding the feet; the right foot leads, with the left foot (in a sliding motion) quickly dragging after. Competition kendo does not allow blows or cuts to the legs.

The belt system in kendo is not the same as in the other martial arts. There are only six kyu grades before the black belt. A white or striped tunic top *(keikogi)* indicates a student or kyu grade; a dark blue top indicates the wearer is a *shodan* or black belt. On average it takes approximately five years to advance from sixth kyu beginner to a first dan black belt.

Once the beginner has learned the basic techniques, he or she advances to the next stage which involves practicing with an opponent. To help a novice get the feel of hitting a real object he or she is introduced to a device called a *knocking post* which also teaches him or her to maintain a well-balanced posture and tight hand grip. The post is not dissimilar to that of the makiwara of karate.

As the kendoka progresses so he or she begins to favor certain methods and techniques according to personality, height, weight, build, and so on. And, as his or her expertise increases, so on occasion will a kendoka fight with two swords – one will be a shinai, of the standard regulation length, the other a much shorter wooden blade. This type of fighting is called *ni to* and requires a great deal of skill and strength. The name derives from Japan's feudal past and the greatest swordsman of all, Miyamoto Musashi (his name means two swords).

Miyamoto Musashi was 13 years old when he killed his first man, a rival fencing master who insulted his father. He went on to fight in over 60 duels, and was only ever beaten once in his life. His conqueror was Muso Gonnosuke, who was the inventor of the four-foot two-inch stick for fighting in *jo jutsu*. Gonnosuke had

Left: *The Emperor's palace guard going through their daily kendo practice. Shinai tips touch, and the bout begins.*
Top: *Two kendo competitors fight each other with all the fury the sport demands.*

Above: *Shinai or bamboo swords crash together and the fighters' heels leave the floor as each attempts to come down with force upon his opponent's head with the shinai.*

previously fought Musashi in a friendly duel and was beaten. Somewhat dejected, he retired to a shinto shrine to meditate where he came up with the idea of using a short stick. He began to experiment with the jo, applying all his martial arts knowledge and eventually devising a system called *shindo muso ryu jodo*. Gonnosuke reapproached Musashi and issued a second challenge which was accepted. But fight as he would, even with two swords, Musashi could not beat the old man.

Musashi created many new concepts in fencing. Although it has been said that he never actually practiced a set style (his technique was styleless) he did originate a special technique for the use of the long and short sword which became known as *niten ichi ryu* (the two-sword style). Musashi was convinced that he was invincible and spent most of his life proving it. Many famous swordsmen of the day took him on, testing his ability with the blade. Eventually he ran out of opponents, his reputation intact. Later, Musashi retired to the mountains to write the classic *Gorin no Sho* (Book of Five Rings). This book is a valuable treatise on mental discipline and is today used by Japan's modern businessmen as a guide to strategy in business transactions. In 1645 Musashi died of natural causes aged 61, having spent the remainder of his life as a recluse.

The Japanese religions of shinto and zen Buddhism left an indelible mark on kendo. The art/sport became a way of attaining inner peace. A kendo master can walk away from a fight, still keeping his dignity and self-respect. Since he knows what he can do, he does not need to prove himself. One of the objects in zen and kendo is ultimately to defeat the ego. There are many different schools of kendo but in the final analysis all offer a path to enlightenment and the unification of the spirit. Some years ago a ninth dan kendo master, Sohei Nakamura, voiced the thought-provoking idea that the kendo practiced within the last decades has no practical use whatsoever. He argued that since the kata taught are linear, any karateka or *aikiist* (practitioner of Aikido) working on circular principles could easily defeat the kendoist.

Another art that uses the sword is *iai do*. This is the method of sword drawing based on the techniques of the more classical *iai jutsu*. It is a martial discipline and is not competitive. In 1620 the art was developed into a do form from the old skill of iai jutsu by Hayashi Zaki Jinsuke, who founded the famous style of the

quick draw sword. Although Jinsuke taught this method in his school, *Muso Shinden Ryu*, it was the last grandmaster of this style, Hyakudo Nakayama, who taught and popularized the fast draw.

To understand iai do, the Westerner ought to compare it with the gunfighting techniques of the American Wild West. Success hinged on speed and accuracy. However, in iai jutsu, from which the discipline of iai do is derived, the emphasis was largely defensive, although it could be used to initiate an attack. The defensive characteristics distinguished iai jutsu from ken jutsu. The earlier schools of sword fighting placed no great importance on the drawing of the blade but rather on its effectiveness when unsheathed.

With the unification of Japan under the Emperor Meiji, the feudal period of Japan was over. An edict from the throne prevented the samurais from wearing swords, and the martial skills that had been bred into them for countless generations, were now being abandoned. The samurais turned to different occupations, and ken jutsu fell into a decline. Japan too began to change – it was now entering the modern era and was hungry for industrialization so that it could catch up with the West.

Left: *A kendo master teaching infants the way of the sword. In Japan kendo is thought to promote etiquette and good breeding, hence children begin learning the art at a very early age.*
Right: *The rice cake is cut as an offering to the Shinto gods before a martial arts display takes place.*

Below: *Master swordsman Yasuji Nakajima brings down his sword to within an inch of Ronald Knutsen's head, demonstrating his control with a live blade.*

Fortunately iai jutsu lived on, not on the battlefield but in private practice sessions. And gradually the combative aspects of the many schools of iai jutsu became absorbed in zen, concentrating on training as a means of developing the mind and body. This concept eventually developed into iai jutsu, becoming iai do.

In iai, as it is more familiarly known, many of the techniques are more aesthetic than practical. And since aesthetic values take precedence over everything else there are no sporting aspects connected with iai do. There is a festival each year at the Temple of the Goblin in Kyoto, where exponents of iai do gather to demonstrate their ability with a sword.

A full iai technique involves a draw and a cut, followed by a quick return to the scabbard. The sword is always worn in the *obi* (belt) with the sharp cutting edge facing upward. This enables the draw and cut to become a single action. All iai schools follow four basic principles of attack which are *nukitsuke* – the actual drawing of the blade – followed by *kiritsuke* – the cut – then comes *chiburi* – the symbolic act of shaking off the blood from the blade, after a successful cut – and finally *noto* – returning the blade into the scabbard.

Left: *Using the naginata with a live blade. All blows are executed in an arc from above. The live blade is forbidden in competition and is replaced by a wooden sword.*
Right: *A kyudo master sights the target and mentally prepares himself for the shoot at a samurai festival in Kyushu, Japan.*
Bottom: *An all-wood sports naginata is used against a wooden sword or bokken. Primarily a woman's weapon, practice with naginata is very popular in Japan today.*
Below: *The sport of naginata-do. The attack area in this demonstration is the man's head. Note the rubber tips for safety purposes.*

The principle behind noto involves sheathing the blade very quickly without having to look down to see what you are doing. Needless to say, only those with perfect technique avoid badly injuring themselves. Novices in iai begin training with a dull-edged blade, only when their technique is flawless, and they can draw, cut and resheath a blade blindfolded, can they start using a sharp blade.

To begin the practice of iai, the swordsman sits back on his haunches. First he bows to his sword, which is lying on the floor in front of him. This respect for a weapon exemplifies the high regard the Japanese hold for the katana (sword). Note that the rituals of iai are extremely important, and that since each move has an important meaning they must be carried out with great precision.

Japanese folklore abounds with stories of great swordsmen who defeated opponents with a single cut of their katana. For the samurai warrior, the sword combined qualities that no other culture gave it. The weapon could be as hard as iron or as soft as satin; and it was more than just a means of defense, it was the symbol that epitomized everything the samurai stood for and believed in. For example,

during the crusades King Richard the Lion-heart encountered the enemy leader Saladin. Richard showed off his sword skills by hacking through an iron bar, and Saladin retaliated by dropping a silk handkerchief across his Damascus steel blade, which instantly halved the fabric in two. The samurais revered the sword, for it incorporates the qualities of both these examples, strength and finesse.

In the same class of the Japanese blade arts is the weapon called a *naginata*. Today it is specifically a woman's weapon. The art of naginata was the martial method of the samurai women. The weapon is similar to that of the western halberd, and the blade was made from the same steel used for the Japanese sword-blade. It is a very powerful weapon when handled skillfully, and is almost as effective as a sword but has a longer reach. For the samurai women, the naginata was not a sport, but an excellent means of defending the home. In fact the samurai women had a reputation as ferocious fighters, and for dying as bravely as the men.

To use the naginata properly, this long pole-like weapon must be twisted through a half circle so that the shaft is used almost as much as is the blade. A series of slashes build up into a potent attack, blows showering down in an arc from above, or scything upward from below.

Before 1945 the naginata had become the most popular form of physical training in Japanese girls' schools. After the war, the use of the naginata almost disappeared as a result of the American ban on weapons. When eventually the ban was lifted all the naginata schools combined to develop a modern form. Traditional naginata was the art of the cut or slash, whereas the modern form adopts the strike as an attack.

In Japan sport naginata is now the most popular women's training in the martial arts. After learning the basic techniques women test each other's skills in competition. To reduce the chances of injury the training weapons have been modified: they have a light split bamboo blade on the end of the shaft; the shaft itself measures about 6 feet 6 inches in length and is made of wood; and armor covers the main target areas, which are the head, neck, shoulders, forearms, trunk and shins. As in kendo, naginata contestants must shout out the name of their target just before they launch an attack, and the judges decide whether it was successful, awarding points to the victor.

In many instances, where female naginata take on male kendoka, they emerge as winners. Since they cannot match the men for strength, they can concentrate on speed and flexibility which, backed up with skill, is a winning combination. In ancient times a shorter naginata was used by the women for use in the home. Bigger weapons were impractical in the traditional Japanese low-ceilinged house.

Use of the naginata on the battlefield dates back more than a thousand years. A warrior armed with such a formidable weapon, which was both blade and staff, had a distinct advantage over the samurai armed with a katana. Not only could it outreach a sword, but also the naginata had a tremendous sweep – if an opponent evaded the razor sharp blade the user could still whip the butt end around to sweep the opponent off his feet, and then decapitate him or her. Because of the naginata's shape and size it presented the feudal warrior with a distinct advantage over the spear *(yari)*.

With the modernization of battlefield weapons the naginata, along with the bow and arrow, fell into disuse. But from the later nineteenth century the naginata reappeared in girls' physical education, and in rituals performed at tea ceremonies.

Another skill which was adopted by women as well as men was that of *kyudo* (the way of the bow). Kyudo, perhaps more than any other Japanese martial art, is directly linked with zen Buddhism and is often called the zen archery of Japan. In kyudo the archer has only one opponent – himself.

The goal in kyudo, like all those in zen, is as elusive 'as trying to catch the wind in your hands.' The ultimate aim is to have no goals at all. A kyudo exponent has to fuse together the bow, arrow and the target in order to become one with them all. At this stage the *kyudoka* (one who practices kyudo) releases the arrow. Even then, hitting the target is secondary. The object of the exercise resides in how well one shoots the arrow and in the archer's state of mind at the moment of release.

Kendo is best summed up by the old saying 'to achieve the proper style in kyudo is to glimpse the mastery of life itself.' The art is executed and performed with a ritualized exactness, to such an extent that very few master the total concept. That is why so few are able to achieve the ultimate knowledge and enlightenment that makes one a master. The archer approaches the target in a semi-medita-

Above: *A Japanese swordmaster slices through a bamboo pole with one clean cut. Great skill is required for a swordsman to be able to achieve this without knocking down the pole. In ancient times, swordsmen tested their blades on condemned prisoners.*
Left: *A line drawing of an early Japanese bowman. The crude bow was replaced in much later years with a finely balanced instrument that was often a work of art as well as a battlefield weapon.*

tive pose, striving to reach the correct state of mind. Even the slightest variation in execution, style, or attitude can result in a total failure if the archer manages to hit the bull's eye, but does it in the wrong frame of mind, then he might just as well have missed the target altogether – such is the exactness of the art. The beauty of kyudo and its value to practitioners in the other martial arts lies in its ability to transcend the values of the fighting arts beyond physical victory.

The bow used in kyudo is unique in Japan – it measures over six feet in length and is the longest bow in the world. The grip is centered approximately one third of the way from the bottom, unlike the centrifugal grip of the other Asian countries. Traditionally the bow was constructed entirely out of bamboo, with a string pull of over 80lb. And because the grip of the kyudo bow is close to the bottom it increases its strength.

The two main schools in existence today are the ogasawara and hekki schools (the latter was a splinter group established in the sixteenth century, which concentrated upon a more practical approach). The ogasawara school developed along ritualistic and ceremonial lines. This style was particularly noted for its very high draw and is the most universally practiced in Japan today.

The act of firing an arrow is divided into eight stages, known as *hassetsu*. First comes *ashbumi*, the archer's tread or step, and the proper stance. The second stage is *dozukuri*, involving upper body positioning, the torso being held straight but relaxed, and controlled breathing. Third is *yugamae*, which is setting the bow in place with the arrow in the firing position. Fourth is *uchiokoshi*, which involves lifting the bow and looking toward the target. The archer then turns his gaze away from the target which is termed respectively *monomi* and *daisan*. Fifth comes the draw, or *hikiwake*. The string hand pulls the arrow all the way back behind the ear. From this stage the archer holds his position while ensuring that all the correct procedures have been observed. This sixth stage is termed *kiai*, or the meeting.

From here on, the archer waits for the arrow to shoot itself, which happens when the strain is too great for the archer's thumb to hold the string. The archer does not willingly release the arrow, it just happens – this is known as *hanare*, or the release. With the arrow in flight the archer waits to see if it reaches the designated spot. Finally, the motionless stance while waiting is called *zanshin*, which means the moment of knowledge.

Many of the weapons used in the Japanese martial arts have their origin in Okinawa. They were originally farming implements, but were made into weapons by the islanders when the occupying Japanese confiscated their bows, guns and swords. Thus the *sai, tonfa, nunchaku* and *kama* were born.

The sai is a short, dagger-like weapon resembling a trident. This three-pronged instrument is about 15-20 inches long and was used as a defensive weapon against the sword and longstaff. Used in pairs, with a spare one tucked into the belt, the first sai can trap a downward blow from a sword while the free hand stabs the samurai with the other sai (the spare could also be thrown at a mounted horseman). Many karateka train in the use of the sai as an extension of their art, all the movements being blocks, thrusts or strikes.

One weapon that has recently become infamous is the nunchaku. This weapon, which can be used like a whip or flail, consists of two lengths of wood joined together either end by a length of cord or chain. However, some people who saw them being used in the Bruce Lee films realized their potential as devastating weapons and forced the authorities to legislate against their use. They were classified as offensive weapons.

The original use of nunchaku was for flailing rice from the husks. Nunchaku, in one form or another, can be seen in many cultures around Southeast Asia. One of the most important aspects of wielding the nunchaku is accuracy and control and if it is handled by an unskilled person it can cause as much damage to the user as to an opponent.

In recent years the nunchaku has been modified into a foam or rubber weapon, of the same length and size as the original, and is used in competitions. This *nunchaku de combat* was pioneered in France. However, the nunchaku is an extremely dangerous weapon and in 1974 the Californian penal code made it an imprisonable offense even to be seen carrying one, let alone fighting with one.

Still in the realms of adapted Okinawan weapons is the *tonfa*, sometimes called the *tui fa*. This was originally the handle of a manually operated millstone for grinding rice. It consists of a long hardwood shaft with a cylindrical grip placed at a right angle, six inches

from the end. Holding this grip, the user can revolve the tonfa to spin outward and strike an enemy in the head. It can also be used with the shaft lying along the underside of the arm to block a sword strike and parry an attack from almost any other weapon.

An American serviceman, while serving in Okinawa in the late 1960s, witnessed a village policeman quell a riot using such an implement. Taking this knowledge back home with him, he developed the tonfa and redesigned it to the same length as a police baton but constructed it out of black glassfiber instead of wood. This new weapon was named the PR 21 prosecutor baton. Within five years of its introduction to the United States virtually every major police force in the world adopted it as standard issue, replacing the old billy club or night stick.

And last but not least is the kama, the sickle used in agriculture. Today it is made from wood (including the blade) and again plays an important part in the karateka's training. Yet in times of strife, especially in Okinawa, the sickle or kama was put to deadly use. Once its metal, crescent-shaped blade was honed to razor sharpness, they were used in pairs to attack the invading Japanese. A fully armored soldier could be decapitated with one blow. The kama was also used in a hooking combination to parry attacks from the samurai with either sword or lance. Today, when a kama demonstration is given, the user wears the *hakama*, or split skirt, for purely ritualistic purposes.

The Japanese martial artist has a wide range of weapons, from short sticks to poles of varying lengths, each of which has its own discipline, tradition, kata, and working technique. As if to emphasize the sheer number of weapons, there is a statue at Nara, in Japan, of a Buddha with 1000 hands. Each hand holds a weapon that, at one time or another, was used on the battlefields of Japan's turbulent feudal era. The extraordinary ability of the oppressed to turn so many objects into weapons has left today's martial artists with a legacy that cannot be matched anywhere else in the world.

Left: *Women archers raise their bows while keeping their eyes on the target. In kyudo aim is less important than the archer's state of mind. When the correct mental attitude is achieved the arrow will be released. The quality of the act takes precedence over everything else.*

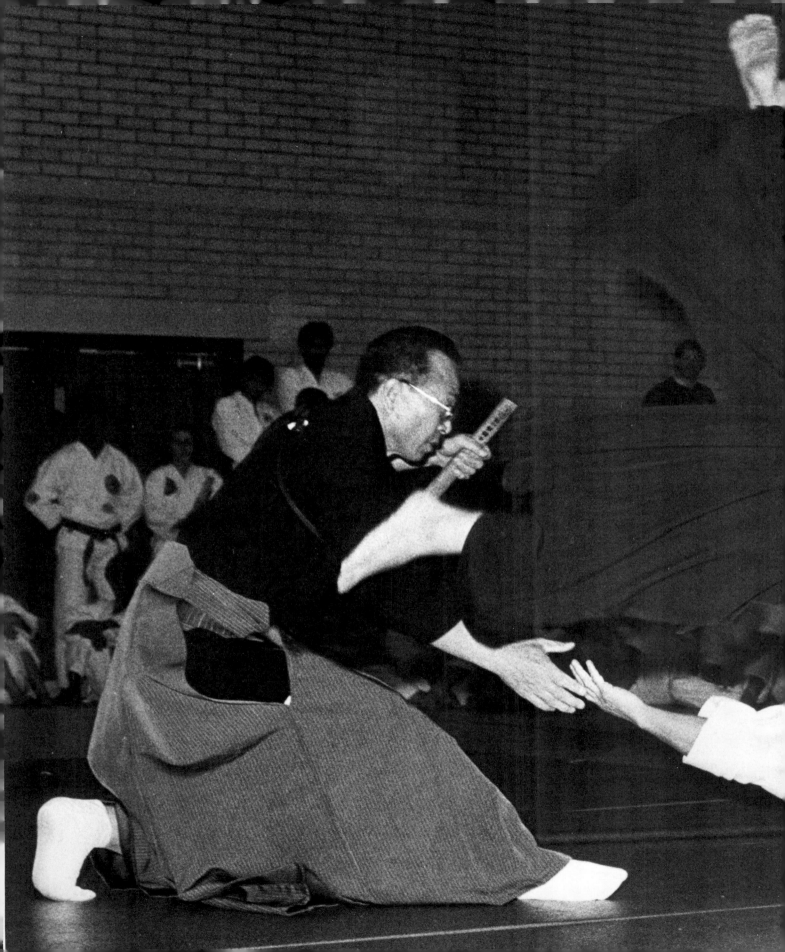

JAPANESE UNARMED ARTS

A single false move loses the game

Using bodyweight and circular movement, this jujitsu master is able to throw a full-grown man over his shoulder and to the ground with one hand.

The Japanese grappling arts are nearly 1000 years old. Of the many unarmed defense systems in existence none is stranger than *sumo* wrestling. This strictly indigenous art-cum-sport is unique to Japan. It is believed that sumo is more than 2000 years old, with its origins stretching further back into folklore and mythology.

Steeped in ancient legends and the shinto religion, sumo wrestling was officially sanctioned in 1684, having previously been known as *kanjin zumo*. When sumo became a professional martial art and sport, a series of rules and regulations were drawn up, and each town and village boasted at least one professional *sumotori* (the correct term for a wrestler).

In feudal Japan the best sumo fighters were given virtual samurai status by the lords and within 100 years sumo wrestling became a national sport. But like so many of the martial arts of Japan sumo wrestling temporarily fell into decline with the Meiji restoration. The wrestlers, who only knew how to fight, had to become bodyguards of rich merchants, and doormen in the Yoshiwara (red-light district) brothels of Tokyo.

Then, in 1889, after much petitioning to the government, sumo wrestling was finally reinstated as a sport and the Tokyo Ozumo Kyokai was born (Tokyo Sumo Association). With new interest in the national sport sumo wrestling grew from strength to strength and it is still governed by the same body.

Although, traditionally only the Japanese can become sumotori, Jesse Kahualua (a Hawaiian with Japanese grandparents) broke into the ranks of wrestlers and became very famous. Fighting under the name of Takamiyama, he climbed right to the top of the sumo tree to become a grand champion or *yokozuna*. Once the yokozuna class is reached, the wrestler continually has to demonstrate his

Right: *Two sumotori about to enter battle. Both have their fists clenched, indicating that the next move will be a head-on clash.*

Below right: *The wrestler in the crouched position has successfully pushed his opponent over the rope ring, thus making him the winner.*

Below: *Two mighty sumo wrestlers locked in combat. Legend relates that the first sumo bout took place when the god Takemika-zuchi fought a rival for the possession of land.*

superiority by winning his *shobu* (bouts). Should he lose more than eight matches or bouts the unwritten code stresses that he must voluntarily retire from wrestling forever.

The sumotori's familiar topknot hair style, the traditional hallmark of the warrior, is not worn until the wrestler reaches the *maku uchi* division, which is one of the two top categories. The wrestler's hair is never cut until he retires from active fighting.

Since the art is steeped in shintoism (the indigenous animistic religion of Japan), fighting, or *basho*, is surrounded by ceremony and ritual. These fights are surprisingly brief, the majority being over in less than one minute. A fighter always begins a contest by stamping his feet to drive away the evil spirits in the ring (the sumotori are very superstitious). Wrestlers fight virtually naked save for a loincloth garment known as a *mawashi*, which resembles a huge baby's nappy. The mawashi is a heavy piece of silk measuring more than 10 yards in length and is folded into four segments, being wrapped around the waist and groin.

Sumo fights take place in a *dohyo*, a dirt mound covered in sand measuring 15 feet in diameter. The whole area is unroped and the object of the sumotori is simply to eject his opponent from the ring. The methods the sumotori employs to this end include tripping, throwing, pushing and pulling. He wins if any part of the opponent's body goes beyond the ring. Although the fight lasts for less than a minute the preparation can take anything up to half an hour, as the time-honored rituals are observed to the last detail. It is this religious aspect of the fight that has resulted in the relative unpopularity in the West.

When a fighter enters the dohyo he begins the ceremony by scattering salt in the ring to purify it. A priest is always on hand to ensure that the customary rites are correctly observed. The salt throwing takes at least four minutes, and incredibly the audience judges the fighter on how well he does this rather than on his fighting attributes. Because of the importance of Shinto rituals in sumo matches, the more important bouts take place at shrines.

Once the ceremonial niceties have been observed, the two sumotori assume a crouching position and, at the referee's signal, charge each other, meeting in the center of the ring with a resounding smack. This is the moment of truth. Some great fights have lasted little more than five seconds. To grasp the strange

Above: *Under the careful eye of the instructor young Japanese boys wearing the traditional loin cloth and waist band get to grips with each other, learning one of the many holds involved in the sport. The sport has become so popular in recent years that schoolboy leagues have been established.*

Top: *A wrestler throwing salt into the ring before the fight as an act of purification, one of many time-consuming rituals to which the sumotori adhere.*
Top right: *Professor Morihei Ueshiba, the founder of aikido.*
Right: *Using aikido women can overcome even the strongest of men.*

hold sumo has on its millions of fans, new-comers to the sport ought to immerse themselves in the Shinto religion and understand the Japanese mentality. At a tournament the referee assumes an unusual role. His word is absolute law, and neither wrestler has any right of protest. And there is no such thing as a tie.

Not surprisingly, the prime requisite of a sumotori is strength and stability. The average sumo weighs on average 350lb, with most of this being concentrated around the lower part of the body. The sumotori live on a diet of very rich food and undertake a series of special exercises to help to put on this enormous weight. The ultimate aim is to produce thick legs, and heavy hips and stomach which in turn create a low center of gravity. This gives the wrestler good balance and stability.

Professional sumo is divided into six divisions, with further subdivisions. Progress to the very top is entirely a matter of skill.

Sumo wrestling is a far cry from the unarmed arts that later developed in Japan. These disciplines followed the lines of the warrior arts that eventually became martial ways and even sports.

Aikido means the way of harmony, and was founded by Morihei Ueshiba. As a child he was so ill with scarlet fever that he was severely debilitated. In an effort to regain his strength Ueshiba began training in the *yagyu shinkage ryu* style of jujitsu. Within a few months his ability and strength increased tremendously so that at the outbreak of the Russo-Japanese war a few years later he was conscripted into the army. During this period Ueshiba saw many different martial arts, and began studying combat methods in earnest. When the war ended he returned to jujitsu and was made a master instructor.

Ueshiba went on to learn other styles of jujitsu but became increasingly dissatisfied with the then-current militaristic styles. When, in 1920, his father died he was so distressed that he sought spiritual guidance from a priest of the Omoto Shinto sect, named Deguchi. With Deguchi's aid Ueshiba meditated, and had a vision of enlightenment in which he floated, bathed in a golden vapor. Others have interpreted this experience as a *satori*, or enlightenment, which is usually achieved after meditation. Ueshiba interpreted his vision as meaning that the fundamental principle of the martial arts is universal love, and not combat. At this moment in his vision Ueshiba had

Left: *Morihei Ueshiba, the grand old man of aikido, demonstrates his art at the opening ceremony of the newly completed practice hall of the aikido headquarters in Shinjuku, Tokyo, Japan.*
Right: *A jujitsu teacher causes a student excruciating pain by applying a simple wrist lock.*
Center right: *A jujitsu arm lock can control an attacker with ease. With one slight movement the holder can break the attacker's arm.*
Far right: *This simple back arm lock is used by many law-enforcement agencies to control prisoners, and is very effective.*

looked into the universal flow, and his mind and the universe were one. He saw that the true martial arts were not about brute force but harmony and *ki* (Ki is an intrinsic energy, known in China as *chi*. It is the ki in the martial art aikido.) This great revelation dramatically changed Ueshiba's view of the martial arts, and was the informing spirit behind aikido.

Ueshiba's newly formulated fighting principle of harmony and gentleness was put into practice when he opened his first dojo in Tokyo in 1927. He taught his students that being passive is the correct defense and that it is necessary to blend with an opponent, entering this aggressive energy before turning it against him. So, if an opponent is going to pull, do not pull against him but pull with him. Whereas in jujitsu and judo the defender waits for an attack to come to him, aikido involves not being there at all at the moment of attack. Since Ueshiba is a pacifist there are no strikes in aikido. And unlike the other martial arts there is a relaxed atmosphere. The emphasis is on peace and harmony, which reigns supreme above all else.

But to find the very essence of the art, one must look far deeper than just applied techniques. The one word that keeps recurring is *ki* and without an understanding of it aikido would be reduced to a series of locks and holds and nothing else. Ki is the source of energy that allows practitioners to perform the impossible, to defy the natural laws of science and to execute tremendous physical feats. It is a kind of super power that knows no bounds, a universal life force inside each of us that is just waiting to be released. One method of doing so involves concentration and special breathing techniques.

Demonstrations of this awesome power have been witnessed on many occasions by the media. Ueshiba's top student, a man named Koichi Tohei, had arrows fired at him from a distance of less than 20 feet. He warded them off as if he was swatting flies. Not one arrow even touched him. On another occasion the master himself, then 85 years old, allowed six black belts to attack him. When they did he summed up his ki energy and tossed them about the dojo as if they were rag dolls. Other such feats involved Ueshiba inviting several black belts from other martial arts to see if they could push him over. The old master centered his ki energy through his stance to become immovable. Try as they would the black belts failed in their attempt to overcome this old man, just 5 feet tall and weighing less than 125lb. Feats like this defy explanation, but they happen time and time again in aikido.

  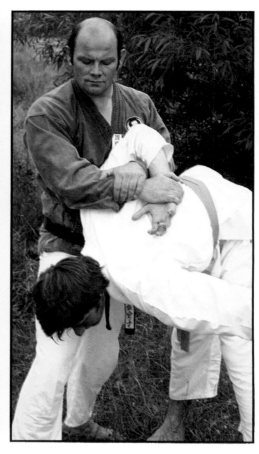

The working principle of ki is that it moves in circles which are not limited but expand to infinity. But the *aki-ist* (one who practices aikido) is forbidden to use a linear approach because, although it can generate a tremendous force, it is self-destroying when used against circular motion. Understanding the philosophy of life is an important factor in the study of aikido. The art teaches adepts to master the mind, develop the character and cultivate the art of living harmoniously.

All the ancient Japanese traditions suffered a traumatic shock when the Emperor of Japan surrendered at the end of World War II. The new American administration of Japan considered that the martial arts encouraged militaristic behavior and banned their practice. Instead, the Japanese were encouraged to take up American sports such as baseball which caused a widespread cultural revolution. Many of the younger Japanese were no longer content to accept that the most vital ingredients of the martial arts were philosophy and religion, and many of the old forms (including aikido) were turned into sport. After 1949 aikido divided into two main schools. One followed Ueshiba's method, the other incorporated fighting contests. This is called *Tomiki sport aikido*, after the master who developed it.

Kenji Tomiki founded the only aikido system that was sports orientated. Tomiki was a student of Ueshiba's and disagreed with the founder's principle that aikido should be noncompetitive.

Another style of aikido is *Yoshinkan aikido*, whose founder was Gozo Shioda. Shioda had trained with the great master for more than 20 years. In the early 1950s Shioda gave a demonstration to the Tokyo police in unarmed combat, using the main techniques of aikido. They were so impressed that they signed him as their trainer; two years later he opened his own dojo. Although spiritually Yoshinkan aikido is still very much attuned to Ueshiba's aikido, it is geared toward combat.

Perhaps the most common of all the Japanese martial arts is the locking and limb twisting art of jujitsu. This art was probably the first to be introduced to the West from Japan, the forerunner of judo and the inspiration behind aikido. It has a vast array of techniques, including attacks against the vital points of the body (*atemi*), joint-locking skills, methods of strangulation and kicking maneuvers. Freely translated, the name means the art of gaining victory by yielding or pliancy, though it is perhaps more commonly referred to as the gentle art.

The art dates back to antiquity, being known in its time as *taijutsu* (body art) and hakuda. Since various throwing arts have existed in Japan for nearly 1000 years it seems likely that jujitsu originated at this time. Later, additional Chinese styles gave it fresh impetus and refined its approach. The many methods that purported to be jujitsu were systematized by Hisamori Takenouchi in 1532.

It must be stressed that jujitsu is not a contest of muscular skill and strength. The art relies excessively on balance, leverage and speed to effect the necessary movements, at which point, strength is applied. And because

Above: *A typical scene from a Japanese dojo. Before beginning each lesson all the students bow to their sensei (teacher) and then to one another as a mark of respect.*
Above, far right: *This maneuver is termed the lift foot pull sweep. The technique involves kicking one of the opponent's feet out from under him, and lifting his foot upwards to unbalance him.*
Left: *Jujitsu grandmaster 18th in line soke (the head of a system or style), Tsuyoshi Munetoshi Inouye. This amiable gentleman is equally effective with a sword in his hand.*

leverage is so important, jujitsu tends to wipe out the differences in size, weight, height and reach between opponents, so evening out the odds. Jujitsu is equally accessible to men and women and is potentially far more devastating than its sporting counterpart judo.

Jujitsu incorporates a combination, or a

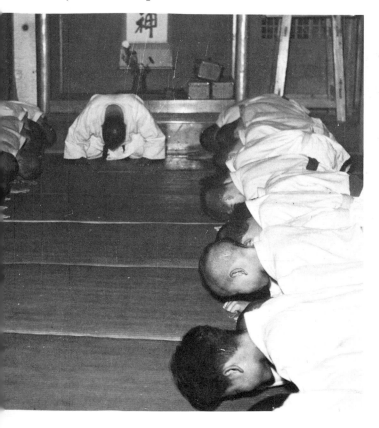

series of combinations, of throws, locks and holds applied to the limbs. They are implemented in such a way that by the addition of extra pressure, dislocation of a joint or an actual breakage can occur. The art is based entirely upon a thorough knowledge of balance, together with an accurate understanding of the body's construction.

The joints of the limbs and body have only a limited movement, whether you are moving backward, forward, sideways or in a circle. They are so delicate that pressure on them creates pain; if it is increased the joints can easily be dislocated. Jujitsu uses a system of holds and locks, and the application of leverage, to put the joints under such intense pressure that an opponent is forced to submit.

At advanced levels of jujitsu students learn *kuatsu*, the ancient art of resuscitation or revival which was once considered the supreme knowledge. At the height of the art's popularity there were as many as 700 different schools each using thousands of techniques aimed at

combating every type of attack. Today's jujitsu probably bears little resemblance to its earlier style practiced in feudal Japan.

An offshoot from one of the popular styles is *small circle jujitsu*, developed by Professor Wally Jay of Almeda in California. It was taught to most of the Western world's special forces during World War II. In particular, American agents from the OSS (Office of Strategic Service) were trained in this Japanese strangulation art for use on operational ventures and covert activities behind enemy lines. Before karate and other, more subtle, martial arts became known to the West, almost all self-defense skills and unarmed combat practiced by their secret agencies stemmed from jujitsu.

By far the most popular martial art (or more correctly sport) in the West is judo (gentle way). Judo is the only martial art to have gained Olympic recognition and boasts over six million active students. It is a well-organized system using unarmed techniques, primarily based on throws using leverage and holds. It was developed partly from the ancient and more lethal skill of jujitsu. Judo has been classed as a fighting art, a spiritual discipline and an excellent form of physical education. The latter was the primary intention of its founder, who believed that healthy individuals created a healthy nation.

Like the founder of aikido, judo's founder, Dr Jigoro Kano, also suffered ill health as a child. Since he was constantly bullied at school he worked out a plan of physical fitness. At the age of 17 he took up the martial arts and trained in jujitsu under Hachinosuke Fukoda, who taught the *tenjin shinyo* school. This particular branch of jujitsu specialized in nerve-point attacks and striking techniques. When his teacher died he enrolled at another school, this time specializing in *nagewaza* (throwing techniques). Then in 1882 Jigoro Kano founded his own style which at first was called *kano-ryu*, but was later changed to *Kodokan judo*.

Kano opened a small school in Tokyo with only nine students but he soon made his name. He was challenged by a local fighter, the great champion Fukushima, and beat him with such little difficulty that his fame quickly spread. Even better, in 1886, a grand tournament was held by the Japanese police force, which invited all the jujitsu schools to take part. Kano went along with a hand-picked team of 15 fighters, who won 13 of their 15 matches, thus establishing their supremacy once and for all. Kano's new art was now recognized by the Butokwai, the governing body for the martial arts. And, in 1964, it became an Olympic sport.

The Kodokan building in Tokyo is, today, the world headquarters for judo. In 1952 an international judo organization, known as the International Judo Federation, was formed to promote international competition. It has over 70 member countries.

The first thing a student learns when he begins judo training is the *ukemi waza* or breakfall. The student is also taught not to let the head hit the ground and how to fall correctly, and to control his hands so they do not fly wildly in the air.

Nearly 80 percent of all judo consists of *randori* (free sparring). Under club conditions, students pair up and practice throwing and grappling. At first, a beginner learns how to yield with the oncoming attack as a palm tree yields to the wind. From here, the student is taught progressively more demanding moves.

In randori judo, players (judo uses the term player rather than fighter) may use whatever methods they like in trying to defeat an opponent, providing that they do not hurt each other and always obey the strict rules of etiquette. Randori free sparring does not use prearranged movements, but consists of spontaneous actions under controlled conditions. Speed is absolutely essential, both in mind and action for unless a player immediately grabs an

Above left: *Competition judo is a hotly contested sport. Here Van de Walle of Belgium goes into the attack. Judo is the only martial art with Olympic status and recognition.*
Left: *Two judo competitors vying to see who can pull the other* *down first during the 1986 Asian games in Seoul, South Korea.*
Below left: *Paul Ajala (Great Britain) versus A Ruggiero (USA) in an International Judo event.*
Above: *The legendary Brian Jacks gets to grips with an opponent.*

advantage the tables could be quickly turned and the vanquisher become the vanquished. An excellent method of self-improvement is fighting a better player to identify and correct your own mistakes and learn from the opponent's technique.

The uniform of the *judoka* is made of a heavy-duty cotton material similar to the uniform of a karateka, but much stronger in construction. It has to be tougher because of the enormous amount of tugging and pulling; a lighter cloth would quickly rip. As in most of the other martial arts, judo uses the colored-belt grading system. Jigoro Kano, the founder, is the only 12th dan in judo's 100-year history.

Since World War II the West has been very successful at this Oriental art and has, on many occasions, beaten the Japanese at their own sport. When judo was first introduced into the Olympics in 1964 in Tokyo, Dutchman Anton Geesink shocked the Japanese people by winning the open title to take the gold medal. In 1972 another Dutchman, Wilhelm Ruska, took two gold medals in the Munich Olympics when he won the heavyweight and open titles.

As we have seen, nearly all the Japanese unarmed fighting and grappling arts have religion at their core. Fighting and worship go hand in hand. In Japan today, there are many fighting arts that are so tied up with religious rituals that one cannot even hope to gain instruction without first entering into holy orders. This is certainly true of the unarmed fighting method of *shorinji kempo*.

Nippon shorinji kempo has been greatly influenced by the Buddhist sect of Kongo Zen. Its followers believe that the only power people should be guided by is knowledge of the world, and that a belief in one god simply divests man of most of his moral responsibility. In Japan alone there are over a million practitioners of this martial art.

Shorinji is the Japanese translation of the Chinese word for Shaolin, and kempo is the translation of the Chinese word for fist. So, the exact translation is the Shaolin fist way. Although it is essentially a modern Japanese martial art, the roots go back to China and the kung fu tradition.

The founder of shorinji kempo was Japanese and named Doshin So. Doshin So was born Michiomi Nakano in 1911 in Okayama Prefecture, the son of a customs officer. Since his father died when he was very young, Nakano was sent to live with his grandfather in Manchuria; who was an employee of the South Manchurian Railway Company. Twelve years later his grandfather died and Nakano returned to Japan. Back home, Nakano came under the guidance of Mitsuru Toyama who had been a close friend of both Nakano's father and grandfather. Toyama is credited with founding the ultra-nationalistic Black Dragon Society (known also as the Amur River Society).

Nakano was recruited into the society and, because of his invaluable knowledge of Manchuria was sent back there to conduct intelligence operations disguised as a Taoist priest. He then placed himself under the tutelage of a senior priest, master Chin Ryo, who was himself a section chief of a secret society known as Zaijiri which had connections with the infamous Chinese Triads. During his travels across Manchuria Nakano found that his master was an expert in a rare style of kung fu called byakuremonken. The young Nakano learned all he could from the old priest, and gradually began to build up and develop a stylized pattern of techniques.

During his period with Chin Ryo, Nakano met other members of the society and learned various kung fu principles. Some years later, while in Peking, Nakano met a man named Bunta So, the twentieth headmaster of the northern Shaolin system of *giwamonken kung fu*, also called *i ho chuan* (the followers of this system reputedly initiated the Boxer Rebellion some years before). Over the following years Nakano spent much time studying the whole system of giwamonken kung fu. In 1936, however, he apparently became the twenty-first headmaster of the style. It is at this point that many historians refute Nakano's claim to the headmastership which is hardly surprising since foreigners did not usually become leaders of Chinese martial arts. Although Nakano, in later life under his new name of Doshin So, insisted that he had been made a headmaster, there is no other proof.

When Russia invaded and captured Manchuria in 1945, Nakano as a Japanese national beat a very hasty retreat aided by secret society members. The following year he was repatriated and returned home to Japan. When he saw the ruins of his homeland and the lack of morals within the populace under the allied occupation, he set about trying to restore national pride in Japan's youth. He began by learning jujitsu and aikido. Then, in 1947, he systematized all his martial arts' knowledge, revising and expanding on the areas he thought relevant. Later, he began a crusade, almost single-handedly trying to build an exact replica of a Shaolin Temple on Japanese soil. He adopted the Chinese rendering of his forename of Michiomi, and called himself Doshin So.

The site Doshin So chose for his great philosophical venture was the small seaport town of Tadotsu. When he arrived with a few followers he found it rife with black marketeering, and virtually the whole economy was under the thumb of the *yakuza* (Japanese gangsters). Training his small band in the martial arts of shorinji kempo, Doshin So cleared the yakuza out of Tadotsu in less than two years. The town's youngsters were so impressed with this tremendous feat that they flocked to join his organization. The order was deliberately kept religious so that the students would never lose sight of the original aim.

The philosophy of Kongo Zen, which is at the root of the shorinji kempo system, focuses on man as an expression and participant in 'the infinite circle of reality.' Kongo Zen recognizes no supreme power; the only power people can turn to for guidance is knowledge. Furthermore, individuals must express their potential through wisdom, strength, courage and love to live life to its best advantage. Kongo Zen maintains that truth is found only in the middle path of harmony, where mind and matter are inseparably united. In the study of shorinji kempo, students or disciples must re-evaluate their former way of life and then strive for a harmonious balance (yin and yang) between physical and mental needs.

The fighting aspects of shorinji are a vehicle for fostering self-development and greater philosophical understanding. Doshin So's guiding principle is 'live half for yourself and half for others.'

Doshin So's system became so successful that within 10 years it had more than a million members in Japan alone. And, because of its Buddhist origins, shorinji kempo has no weapon systems except for a wooden staff or pole.

Shorinji techniques are based on defense, attack being a last resort. An important aspect of the system is the application of pressure to the vital points on the human body. It designates 142 vital points where striking can cause severe pain or even death. A method for regulating the circulation of the blood, called *seiho*, is also practiced. The severe training methods and strenuous exercises create a build-up of lactic acid but the seiho principle, which is a type of breathing-cum-massage technique, relieves the accumulation of acid, lessens tension and creates new energy.

The fighting methods of the system are informed by both hard and soft movements. In all, there are over 700 techniques, which are said to cover every possible means of defending and protecting oneself in virtually any given situation.

Like jujitsu, which Doshin So once studied, shorinji kempo techniques are not determined by strength or size, but by carefully applied scientific principles of body movement. All

Above: *Two adepts of shorinji kempo train with weapons against empty hands. The special breastplate acts as a body protector to prevent injury. The swastika symbol is of ancient sanskrit origin, and has been adopted by the shorinji kempo organization as its badge.*
Right: *A class of young shorinji kempo students watch engrossed as two senior black belts go through an advanced routine. Shorinji kempo has strong quasi-religious overtones.*

students spend many hours practicing *zazen*, a type of seated meditation, to complement their physical training. Shorinji kempo has been kept free from what the followers term 'the egocentric practices of sport' and has been registered with the Japanese government as a religion.

Practice of this martial art in the West mainly involves its philosophy and applied techniques, rather than strict adherence to its religious principles, although zazen is observed. Some critics feel, however, that shorinji kempo is a nationalistic martial art, and that certainly ties in with Doshin So's history.

THE NINJA AND THE ART OF NINJUTSU

Nothing is to be feared, only to be understood

A ninja poses with his sword.

No fighting unit has captured the imagination of the public in recent years like the *ninja*. The legendary black-clad figures who have swept through Japan's turbulent history for nearly 1000 years have left a trail of mayhem and death in their wake. The ninja warrior was probably one of the most deadly fighting machines in the history of the martial arts. He struck out of the shadows of darkness without fear or favor, hiring himself to the highest bidder. Trained from birth in the most lethal skills of the martial arts, the ninja warrior has left a legacy of awesome weapons and techniques that have secretly re-emerged as a means of self-protection and as a way of life.

Ninjutsu is the art of stealth or stealing in, and its practitioners are called ninja. Its exact origins are, however, shrouded in mystery. Ninjutsu is generally thought to have begun around AD 593 during a period of religious and political upheaval in Japan. At this time a great Chinese philosopher, general and military strategist named Sun Tsu wrote a book entitled *The Art of War*. This was a complete treatise and exact science on warfare, covering offensive strategy, pinpointing an enemy's weaknesses and strengths, terrain, the use of spies, guerrilla warfare and vulnerability. At the time, this book was required reading for Chinese intellectuals, which included Taoist priests and Buddhist monks. However, many scholars fell from favor in the Sui Dynasty royal court. They fled the country and sought refuge in the islands of Japan and later settled in the remote regions of Iga and Koga. Here, in the mist-shrouded mountains, they lived their lives as mystics and hermits.

Over the next few hundred years these *yamabushi*, as they were termed, lived in clans in this comparative wilderness practicing their martial arts and meditating. But they were soon disturbed by political events in Japan. After the death of the Prince Regent Shotoku in AD 622 political and religious factions engaged in a bloodthirsty power struggle over whether Buddhism or Shintoism should be the state religion. There was such disorder that the country suffered both politically and economically until a warrior mountain priest (a yamabushi), by the name of En-no-Gyoja, emerged. He tried to restore order by inventing a new way to propagate Buddhism.

This new religious campaign gained such popular support that the aristocracy and court

elite was forced into a showdown with En-no-Gyoja. They were so afraid that this yamabushi would gain power that they attacked and forced his disciples back into the mountains. Now forced to fight against great odds, the yamabushi borrowed freely from the writings of the mountain hermits (which were essentially Sun Tsu's ideas on warfare) and, by stealth, fear, guerrilla tactics and clever maneuvering, the yamabushi defeated the royalist troops who beat a hasty retreat back to the capital. So, for the next few hundred years, the ninja clans remained in their mountain strongholds living their own life in tune with nature and the cosmos.

By the twelfth century little was heard from the rebellious mountain priests. Meanwhile, the central government had become so weak that many factions among the aristocracy were engaged in power struggles. Constant conflicts between the lords and religious leaders, each jockeying for power, provided the perfect setting for spies and assassins intent on getting rid of political adversaries.

The Kamakura period (1192-1333) came to be known as the golden age of ninjutsu. With all the power mongering going on, the ninja and their infamous talents proved to be the right people at the right time. They were hired by the feuding barons to settle their scores. This period was also infamous for its military dictatorship, the Shogunate, and for the great rise to power of the samurai, whose culture was founded on the principles of zen.

During this period about 50 different ninja schools sprang up with their strongholds in the Iga and Koga provinces. The Hattori and Oe clans jointly ruled Iga, while in Koga province, to the north, families such as Mochizuki, Ukai, and Nakai ruled. Each of the clans had its own top-secret ninja techniques, which were handed down through the generations only to other members of the ninja family. For example a technique known as *koppojutsu*, which specialized in bone breaking, was a particular favorite of the Koto clan. The Fudo family were expert in and responsible for the development of the infamous throwing star called *shuriken*. Espionage and covert activities on a huge scale were the hallmark of the Kusunoki clan. The great Togakure ninja were adept with the *shuko*, an implement that was worn on the hands like a glove, and which had sharp metal spikes protruding outwards to help the ninja

Above left: *The ninja field warrior always carried his weapons with him. Seen here are shuriken or pointed throwing stars (often tipped with poison) plus sword, sai, and ninja climbing claws.*
Left: *A ninja using climbing claws to scale an awkward tree. Climbing claws were often used to scale castle walls.*

Right: *Martial artist and ninja enthusiast Sho Kosugi wearing ninja hand claws. Sho Kosugi has made something of a name for himself as a ninja movie star, having appeared in several films and a television series on the subject.*

grip smooth surfaces (it was used for scaling castle walls, and was also used as a weapon).

By the fourteenth century the ninjutsu had developed into a significant and influential political power no longer content to remain in obscurity in the desolate mountains. Their cunning knew no bounds and feared no person, and even the emperor's closest advisers feared for their lives. No one was beyond the reach of these faceless assassins who would strike out of the darkness and cut a man down before he knew what had happened. The ninja had built up a reputation for getting results 100 percent of the time. There was no such thing as a near miss or a failure. If a lord had been singled out, then he was killed. Around this time the ninja left their mountain strongholds en masse to assassinate the opposing *daimyos* (lords), whom they easily defeated. The ninja were in danger of getting out of control and were even setting their sights on the capital.

There then appeared on the scene an ambitious military general who intended becoming shogun. This was Oda Nobunaga, the dreaded hater and avowed enemy of all ninja. In 1579 Nobunaga sent a huge army of samurai to attack the ninja of Iga under the leadership of his son Katsuyori. However, the ninja forces were too clever and soundly defeated the invading samurai. Two years later, in 1581, Nobunaga retaliated by sending another huge force against the ninja, but this time led the army himself which outnumbered the ninja by more than 10 to one. This time the great general's army won through, and in their wake the samurai slaughtered the men, women, and children of the powerful Iga clan. The ninja survivors who managed to escape this massacre fled back to the mountains to regroup, and later began the slow process of training new ninja in spite of a royal decree outlawing them. Yet victory did not last long for Nobunaga – within a year he was murdered in Honniji territory.

His successor, Ieyasu Tokugawa, had to travel to Okazaki castle to take command of his forces. Since the journey would have taken him through the perilous Honniji lands he decided to take a different though equally dangerous route. Ieyasu made an arrangement with the ninja leader Hanzo Hattori, guaranteeing him a safe passage to Okazaki castle by way of the hazardous mountain region of Iga, the heartland of the ninja. The ninja clans regarded this as a way of securing a more stable relationship with the ruling power-to-be. So, with the assistance of the ninja, Ieyasu made the journey safely and, in 1603, became Shogun of all Japan.

For the next 250 years the Tokugawa Shogunate brought peace and civil order to the country, so eliminating the need for the ninja. But the clever Ieyasu had not neglected to hire Hanzo Hattori and his ninja family to protect him and his Shogunate. Hattori organized his ninja into a secret force and elaborate spy system to alert the Shogunate to any political dissent long before it could ever become a real threat. A ninja, dispatched at the right moment, could quickly rid the Shogunate of a political rival.

Over the next two centuries, the deadly ninja that had once been feared throughout Japan were reduced to little more than gardeners and security guards. And their skills declined along with their secret art.

Not all the ninja families disbanded at the start of the Tokugawa Shogunate. Some still remained in the far-off mountains wrapped in a shroud of secrecy, concealing themselves in their cliff strongholds and maintaining their traditional practices. And they only ventured out one or two at a time to perform assassinations. Although isolated, the ninja kept and maintained an intricate espionage system to help them keep abreast of scientific and technological advances.

It seems fairly reasonable to assume that the stealth and assassination arts of the ninja were re-activated in early twentieth-century Japan. It is certainly known that a great intelligence coup resulted in the Japanese victory over the Russians at Port Arthur in the Russo-Japanese war in 1904. And, as Japan emerged as a modern nation, it instituted a tight security service. Again, it is reasonable to assume that ninja skills and experience were instrumental in setting up this modern network of intelligence.

Today, with the tremendous growing interest in Japanese martial arts, the skills of the ninja and their art of ninjutsu have seen a great revival on a worldwide scale. At the beginning of the 1980s even Hollywood caught the ninja bug and produced films and television series centered around the activities of this infamous organization.

Very few authentic ninja still exist in Japan. Yet there is one master still teaching this ancient art, Masaaki Hatsumi, the thirty-fourth grandmaster of the Togakure ninja system. Many Westerners in the last 20 years have sought out this ninja master to seek training guidance. The more notable, who have gone on to become expert instructors in their own right, are Doron Navon of Israel, Stephen Hayes and Robert Bussey, both American. They and the other instructors have seen a great surge of interest in the ninja and the ninja practitioners of the world treble in number over the past two to three years.

Above left: *Ninja master Harunaka Hoshino directs a student's aim. A few well-placed fire arrows could cause havoc in the enemy camp.*
Top: *Dr Masaaki Hatsumi, a bone specialist and the 34th grandmaster of the Togakure ninja system. It is mainly due to* his teachings that ninjutsu has had so many Western instructors and adherents.
Above: *Harunaka Hoshino strikes a classic combat stance armed with a ninja sword. The sword is much shorter and has a straighter blade than the samurai's.*

Above: *Stealth and surprise were the two main weapons of the ninja. An agent would hide for days concealed in undergrowth or in the branches of a tree, then as if out of nowhere he would appear and pounce on his surprised victim.*

Above right: *A ninja used anything he could lay his hands on for a weapon. The simple fisherman's net is adapted to become a snaring device, to entangle a would-be attacker.*

There is also a current ninja boom in the United States. Today's practitioners, however, are not bent upon death and destruction and are often already competent in another martial art. Their sole aim is to gain a greater understanding of the martial systems through the study of ninjutsu, an art that has often been termed 'the complete way of living.'

Ninjutsu is not just involved in fighting techniques, but also parapsychology. Its practitioners deem the art a pattern for living. And, as Hatsumi believes, personal enlightenment can only be achieved through total immersion in the martial tradition as a complete way of living. Although the art of ninjutsu grew up as an outlawed counterculture to that of the accepted samurai society, its philosophies and fighting methods live on.

Formal training for a ninja in the stealth arts began almost from the cradle. From very early childhood, the children of ninja families were taught to be constantly aware of what was around them. And as they grew older so they were educated in the secrets and specialties of their particular clan. From about the age of five their games took on an air of seriousness and utilized simple training exercises. The children were also tested to see if they had any particular skills. Those who did then received a special education that concentrated on developing their innate talents, just as young Russian athletes attend specific schools from a very early age to develop their talents.

In addition, the children played games that developed balance and agility, running up inclined planks and leaping over low bushes. They also hung from tree branches for hours on end to learn self-discipline, and how to endure pain. Massage was also a vital part of their upbringing, keeping their muscles in good shape and their bones and joints flexible. In later life, should they be captured on a mission and tied up, they could dislocate their limbs and escape.

One of the classical nine exercises for developing stamina and improving running speed involved placing a straw hat on the young ninja's chest. He would start running, initially holding it in place, until he went so quickly that the wind kept it pressed to his chest. However, if the hat fell to the ground the ninja had to keep trying until he passed the test. Tests like this helped the ninjas allegedly run more than 75 miles without stopping.

Ninja training was gruelling. The children

were taught how to squeeze through near impossible openings, hold their breath for long periods underwater and swim great distances at top speed. And their ability to dive from great heights would have been the envy of today's high-board Olympic stars. The ninja were also trained to swim through the water silently, causing barely a ripple. Swimming was not only a vital way of approaching an enemy, but also of escape, and the ninja were taught at what depth they had to swim to avoid arrows, spears and even musket balls.

The breathing methods that were taught were very similar to those of Indian yoga, which is probably where they came from. These techniques enabled the ninja to breathe quietly and slowly, instead of panicking and gulping for air when hiding and being tracked down. Some ninja were capable of reducing their breathing to an absolute minimum by entering into a yoga-induced trance for as long as was necessary. At higher levels of advanced training the ninja could even detect how many people were sleeping in a room, just by listening to their breathing. They learned to distinguish the rhythm of a light from a heavy sleeper, and also a false from a genuine sleeper.

The ninja also learned how to become actors so that they would not be found out when spying and wearing disguises. The repertoire of disguises included priest, merchant, farmer and even beggar which furthermore require a detailed knowledge of these lifestyles and professional skills. So if a ninja had to disguise himself as a priest he had to know what his religious duties would be. Such attention to detail was vital for a successful mission, and could easily be the difference between life and death.

The ninja's life was spent in isolation in the mountains, perfecting such techniques. Ninjas trained everyday for the better part of 20 years. Even after this they would still be learning new techniques as technology changed.

The name ninjutsu means stealing in art, thus a ninja had to be expert in creeping about stealthily. Expertise in this was a result of 10 basic techniques, which are:

1. Nuki ashi – stealthy step
2. Suri ashi – rub step
3. Shime ashi – tight step
4. Tobi ashi – flying step
5. Kata ashi – one step
6. O ashi – big step
7. Ko ashi – little step
8. Kakizami – small step
9. Wari ashi – proper step
10. Tsune ashi – normal step

master, they also had to be expert in camouflage, weapons, pharmacology and dialects. The latter was particularly necessary when operating in different provinces. Living this rugged life as a self-imposed social outcast, the ninja also learned to acclimatize the body to all seasonal extremes. In the winter months they would wear a white uniform to become nearly invisible in the snow. At night, the garb would be changed for black.

Over the years, the ninja legend grew. Superstitious country folk even believed that these assassins could disappear at will. The ninja, realizing the psychological impact of such exaggeration, encouraged these wild stories. But there was no exaggerating when it

Another way the ninja moved stealthily was known as sideways walking or *yoko-aruki*. By moving the legs sideways in a cross-step fashion, the ninja confused the enemy because the tracks do not reveal in which direction the ninja is travelling. They were trained to step carefully and lightly. One method of learning this walk involved laying wet rice paper on the floor and then walking over it but without letting it stick to the soles of the feet.

Since the ninja best operated at night, their eyes and the ability to see well in the dark was crucial. To help them do this the ninja spent hours in small dark rooms letting their eyes grow accustomed to the dark. So when, in later years, they went out on night missions they had little difficulty in seeing in the dark. And as if these skills were not enough for the ninja to

came to the number of weapons the ninja carried. They were walking arsenals and their array of weapons was the most awesome ever assembled at any one period in Japanese history. The ninja only used weapons that were extremely effective, light and concealable. And everything had to be carried within the folds of the *shinobi shozoku* (ninja uniform).

The ninja sword, sometimes referred to as *shinobigatana*, was one of the most important weapons. The sword had a very different meaning for the ninja than it did for the samurai. As we have already seen, the reverence given to the sword of the samurai was nothing short of worship. The ninja's weapon, on the other hand, was shorter than the samurai's katana, measuring 24 inches in length with a *saya* (scabbard) that was two to three inches longer. This saya was more than just a sheath for holding the sword in place. The empty space at the bottom was used for storing explosives, blinding powders, and special tablets for stemming the appetite. It also had a removable tip that, once removed, left a hollow tube for the escaping ninja to breath through while hiding underwater.

Top left: *Stephen K Hayes, the US ninja instructor, is known as the father of Western ninjutsu. He studied under Hatsumi himself.*
Inset left: *The ninja sword. The very long cord on the scabbard was used to strap the sword to the ninja's back. It was also used for tying up prisoners, strangulation, and as an aid for climbing.*
Below right: *Stephen K Hayes adopts a posture for throwing the 'whispering stars of death,' the shuriken.*
Right: *Victor Ferrer of the koga ryu ninja system uses a kusari gama (sickle and chain) to entangle and then dispatch a sword-wielding assailant.*

The blade of the sword was of very poor quality, with an edge that was dull in comparison to the razor-sharp sword of the samurai. The ninja regarded it as just another tool of the trade. The shorter blade enabled him to draw his sword indoors and fight at close quarters which was something the samurai could not do with their larger weapons in the traditional, low-ceilinged rooms. The final difference between the two was that the ninja carried his sword on his back, not hanging from the waist.

Staffs, sticks, canes – all were used by the ninja to defend his life. One favorite weapon was the *kusarigama*. This was a sickle attached to a length of chain or cord with a weight at the far end. The weighted end was thrown at the enemy or could entangle an attacking samurai's sword, at which point the sickle was used to decapitate the opponent.

Probably the most infamous weapon of the ninja's arsenal was the *shuriken* – a small, star-shaped throwing device. Although commonly seen in the shape of a star, the shuriken in fact came in many different shapes and sizes. A ninja concealed nine of these in his clothes, nine because the number had a special mystical significance. The shuriken could be used up to distances of about 30 feet. They were not actually designed to kill outright, but were

quite capable of doing so, particularly when the ends were tipped with a poisonous substance. The ninja's range of weapons was limited only by ingenuity and imagination. Many of the weapons were closely guarded secrets within each school and, when most of the clans died out, so too did their secret weapons.

A typical ninja clan was organized along strict military lines. The whole system was divided into three distinct ranks. At the top of the tree were the *jonin* (leaders), then came the *chunin* (subleaders), and finally the *genin* (the ninja agent). The jonin maintained an extensive intelligence network and made contact with the warlords and daimyos who needed spies or assassins. Once a job had been established, it would be given to the chunin, who selected the field agent to carry out the mission and make all the necessary preparations for a successful mission.

Once a mission had been undertaken, the ninja would not return until the task had been completed. Or, failing that, he would die in the attempt. No matter how adverse the weather conditions or the terrain, the ninja went unerringly for the target. In fact, he often welcomed thunderstorms, earth tremors (Japan has many) and blizzards, taking advantage of whatever nature threw at him since it could distract his opponents. Verbal weapons, such as flattery and jealousy, were also used, to turn neighbor against neighbor, and to glean vital pieces of information. By flattery he could cajole news of important troop movements from vain, petty officials. In the guise of a wandering priest, who in those days also took the news from community to community, he could spread lies to the farmers and villagers. Such subversion was perhaps the icing on the cake.

The ninja clans used women as well as men for their nefarious activities, but in much subtler ways. The ninja women were called *kunoichi* and initially received the same training as the men but, as they grew older, concentrated on developing their feminine wiles. The kunoichi used sex as a weapon, learning the erotic arts to get close enough to a man to kill him. The powerful daimyo, whose life was always under threat, was so wary of the kunoichi (who could easily gain entrance to his inner chambers disguised as a masseuse, prostitute, dancer or singer) that he only allowed his faithful samurai retainers to be close to him.

Above: *A ninja was capable of blending in with his surroundings. Rather than just hide behind an object, the ninja learned how to blend himself with that object, to become virtually invisible.*

Right: *To his enemies, the ninja was often no more than a shadow, striking without warning. Stories of their secret powers led the common country folk to believe that the ninja were ghosts or demons.*

When a mission had been completed, the ninja would head back home. On many occasions soldiers were in hot pursuit so, in order to shake them off, a ninja used his knowledge and skills of camouflage to hide in the terrain. This ability to disappear into his surroundings and his ingenious use of storms, fog and other natural phenomena to escape gave rise to legends claiming the ninja could become invisible at will and were servants of the devil. The suspected presence of a ninja operating in an area could easily strike terror into the bravest of hearts. And if the pursuing forces did manage to corner a ninja in a barn, for example, they would rather burn it to the ground than risk entering and having to fight it out to the death. For his part, the ninja would hide under the floorboards or dig a hole and cover himself with earth. If, when the fire had died out, the soldiers could not find the remains of the ninja among the ashes, they would simply assume that he had become invisible and had escaped, leaving behind the buried ninja to surface when it was safe.

Right: *There are five attitudes in ninjutsu, each represented by a secret finger sign. These signs symbolize (left to right) earth, water, fire, and wind. By forming and concentrating on the most suitable signs, the ninja is able to adopt the correct frame of mind for a particular venture.*

Much of the ninja art is informed by esoteric ideas which provide the basis for and understanding of their unique approach to life. They, more than any other sect, were at one with their environment. Ninja and the art of ninjutsu is a total way of life in which nature and man's own consciousness merge to provide a life that is at one, and in harmony with the universe.

Over several centuries their theories of the occult were developed to unite their mental powers with supernatural forces. The ninja also studied different yoga systems. They devised a method for concentrating all the will and energy into a particular endeavor at a particular time. This superior kind of power was summoned by the adepts who, in a trance-like state, concentrated all their energies upon finger-knitting patterns. The various patterns were known as the five manifestations and represented earth, water, fire, wind and void. While in this trance the practitioner could induce physiological changes including a slowing down of blood pressure and heart beat. An experienced ninja could even change his inhalations and exhalations to such an extent that he could 'shallow breath,' which he occasionally used to feign death.

These finger-knitting patterns were informally referred to as *kuji-in*, or energy channelling. In all, there are 81 such hand maneuvers covering every circumstance that the ninja might find himself in. It is believed that because of the ninjas' early isolation, long meditative practices and mystical teachings, they developed their inherent powers of psychic perception: And, through this increased sensitivity, they were able to extend their mental awareness beyond the five senses. Ninjutsu techniques often incorporated natural symbols as a source of inspiration.

The *go dai*, or five manifestations, were further advanced with the *go gyo* or five elements, which describe how elements inter-

relate and operate. The table of the go gyo is:

Chi – earth

Sui – water

Ka – fire

Moku – wood

Kin – metal

These elements continuously work and interact to create and then destroy each other. For instance, water feeds the growing tree, which is then felled by the metal axe, consumed by fire, and finally scattered in ashes. These five elements can also be seen as they regulate an individual's health and in the unfolding of life's events. The ninja used this knowledge to develop the art of *goton po*, a method of escape and concealment that uses these five elements. Much of this mystical knowledge stems from northern India and Tibet, and later became known as the *mikkyo* (secret doctrines).

The principle behind the *kuji-in* finger-knitting exercise was that it enabled the ninja to transform an idea or desire into reality. Focused intent becomes completed action itself and cause blends with effect until the distinction fades. This ability is vital for combat, since it provides the ninja with power or energy that defies normal physical laws.

The intention-focusing method does not create extra energy, but rather removes the limits that restrict the amount of energy available to an individual. The body is capable of performing the technique, the mind understands what has to be done, and the will ensures that the task is completed successfully.

The awesome power created within the ninja's mind helped create a near superhuman. He has often been termed the ultimate survivor because of his ability to live off the land and cope adequately without any equipment. Surviving in the outdoors against the worst conditions when lesser mortals would be

Left: *The beginning hand position for forming void, the fifth attitude of ninjutsu.*

Below: *The ninja in full costume. Most ninja had reversible suits, with white insides to blend in with the snow.*

doomed was the ninja's specialty. The ninja also had to be able to live for indefinite periods in the wilderness. Sometimes, however, his plans failed and he would have to travel many miles out of his way to escape his pursuers. And if his rations ran out he would have to live off the land for weeks on end. But whatever happened, no matter how unexpected or awful, the ninja was trained to survive.

If a ninja was captured he would first be stripped of his weapons and then locked up. Despite this, it was still the ninja's duty to escape and complete his mission, using make-shift weapons. Such devotion to duty made the ninja warrior a feared and frightening enemy. The ninja also had to be a master of toxins concocted from local herbs. He knew every plant and shrub in the forest, in particular those which offered the most dangerous poisons. His knowledge of chemistry and botany put him on a par with a modern-day pharmacist. Although the ninja did not have access to the sophisticated man-made poisons of today, his knowledge of the organic ones was unrivalled. One of his favorite potions for instant death was a poison extracted from a Japanese fish called the fugu, or blowfish. Under normal circumstances the fugu is con-sidered, even today, a great delicacy, but in certain conditions it is a fatally poisonous fish containing the poison tetradoxin in every organ. It is potentially so dangerous that in Japan today licensed chefs have to have government authorization before they can open a fugu restaurant. Even when cooked for a long period the poison remains virulent and can cause death.

If a ninja wanted to poison someone at a feast, nothing could be more appropriate than a few slivers of fugu slipped onto the victim's plate. The effect would be devastating for the poison attacks the respiratory system at the center of the brain, paralyzing the muscles relating to breathing. The victim dies an agonizing death.

The ninja were also trained to live off the land, surviving on berries and tree roots, and nuts and insects. If he became ill or was wounded, he knew that certain types of mushrooms growing in the forest, such as the puffball fungi, would heal his infected wounds with their antibiotic properties. And should he ever become lost, then he could turn not to a compass or map, but nature and the heavens. An excellent way of pinpointing the south involved looking at a felled tree stump and examining the rings of the grain. Since these rings always grow biggest and peak in a southerly direction, he would immediately know which direction to take.

But what marked out the ninja was the fact that the field agent, or *genin*, even after the long years of exhaustive training, was deemed expendable. The ninja, like the samurai, had no fear of death. And his life was always in his own hands; the skillful lived, the failures were caught, tortured mercilessly and then put to death very slowly. Yet no matter how cruelly they were punished, a code of honor prevented anyone from betraying a colleague. The ninja had to swear on a blood oath of secrecy never to reveal the tactics of the art or the location of the mountain strongholds. And if a ninja was disloyal to the clan he was ruthlessly hunted down by the clan, caught and put to death in the most agonizing manner.

One of the greatest and most infamous ninja leaders of all time was Sandayu Momochi, who operated in the Iga region during Japan's stormy sixteenth century. In order to confuse his enemy and conceal his identity, Sandayu maintained three separate homes, each with a wife and family. When things got too hot for him in one area, he would move to another house and assume a different identity. He kept this ruse up all his life and was never caught. Even when Oda Nobunaga sent his 46,000 troops against Sandayu's 4000-strong ninja army in 1581, all of whom were slain, Sandayu still escaped by assuming one of his different identities and resumed life as a ninja.

Over the centuries stories about the ninja have been exaggerated beyond belief so that separating fact from fiction has been a monumental effort for martial arts' historians.

Western interest in the Japanese martial arts has brought the ancient skills of the ninja and their art of ninjutsu to the surface. Modern-day

Above: *To the ninja no place was inaccessible. He would wade mighty rivers, cross barren lands and scale great heights in order to fulfill his mission.*
Above right: *English ninja instructors Peter King and Keith Libahan engage in ninja unarmed combat.*

Above, far right: *Stephen K Hayes entangles a swordsman with his rope and blade weapon (kusari gama). Once the blade is trapped, the ninja moves in and kills his opponent with the sharp-bladed gama (sickle).*

training for both Western and Japanese students consists mainly of the ninja's methods of unarmed combat, termed *taijutsu* (skill with the body). Although a ninjutsu student is encouraged to learn the esoteric doctrines of the art, he has to begin by mastering the preliminary concepts first.

Taijutsu forms the basis for all understanding in the fighting arts of ninjutsu. The students begin by developing their natural bodily responses, and then progress to using these lessons as models for tactical training. Learning breakfalls and body tumbling methods are also an essential part of the training program.

Many of the popular martial arts' training systems attempt to mold the students' ways of reacting and moving into a stylized set of

predetermined movements. In one way they try to add to the students' total personality. But ninja taijutsu takes the opposite course. It strives to make all movements natural by culminating any awkward or unnatural tendencies that the student may have acquired. As a fighting system taijutsu relies on natural body strength and resilience, speed of response and movement, and an understanding of the principles of nature to guarantee self-protection.

Ninja taijutsu stresses the use of body dynamics, which is the principle of using the whole of the body as a weapon. The fighting stance is always determined by the fighter's relationship to his opponent – there is no predetermined stance. However, absolute beginners are not left completely to their own devices; there is a special pose which sees them through their early lessons. They are also taught four fighting positions, but these are only used as a framework to understand the principles of taijutsu.

These four positions are: natural stance, defensive stance, offensive stance, and receiving stance. In combat, the practitioner stands in a relaxed manner with his arms and legs spread wide apart, as though he were about to give in. As the fight begins, the

taijutsu practitioner seems to vanish, but then suddenly rises up behind the attacker, having neatly side-stepped and outmaneuvered the opponent.

Taijutsu has no sporting form, and is strictly a combat martial art. It aims to inflict the greatest possible damage with the fewest moves and easiest methods. The art involves grappling, throws, escapes, locks, chokes, and muscle and bone attacks. If there is a secret to successful taijutsu, it is efficient and effective movement tied in with perfect co-ordinated rhythm. Since body conditioning is an integral part of taijutsu, the student learns a series of exercises enhancing the elastic qualities of the muscles and joints. The exercise program avoids straining or tearing the muscles, as often happens in the other martial arts. These exercises generate strength through flexibility.

There are thousands of ninja taijutsu techniques, including countless variations on a given theme. Students are not expected to learn all of them but rather to work upon a selection and adapt them to suit their own specific needs. Ninjutsu training has so evolved that it includes techniques for coping with practically any situation. Ninja taijutsu involves living life through a martial discipline, and which reputedly has the answers to everything.

TAEKWONDO AND THE MARTIAL ARTS OF KOREA

Do not despise the snake because he has no horns for one day he may become a dragon

Of all the Asian martial arts it is to Korea we must look for the most exciting and devastating kicking techniques.

Taekwondo (way of the hand and foot) is a version of fighting, taken originally from an ancient Korean unarmed combat method. This martial art is very much a modern concept, but with roots stretching back almost 2000 years to the indigenous native style of *tae kyon*. The name taekwondo came into being at a conference of masters in 1955 when General Choi Hong Hi submitted this particular name because it closely resembled the old name of tae kyon.

Right: *A young taekwondo student executes a flying kick to get over the initiated attack by his opponent.*

Right: *This superb example of a roundhouse kick is indicative of the high-impact kicks that have made the art of taekwondo so popular. In Europe karate tends to dominate the martial arts scene, whereas in the United States nearly 70 percent of all martial arts practiced have a taekwondo origin or background.*
Far right, below: *Two practitioners execute a poomse or pattern, the solo training exercise which is the taekwondo equivalent of the kata of karate or the forms of kung fu.*

The considerable Japanese martial arts' influence on taekwondo is a consequence of their occupation of Korea from 1907-45. Since then the art has developed into a modern international sport and in July 1980 the International Olympic Committee decided to include it in the next Olympic Games, to be held in Seoul, Korea, in 1988.

In the southern part of the Korean peninsula just over 2000 years ago there was a small kingdom called Silla. This kingdom was constantly being attacked by its two more powerful northern neighbors Pak-je and Koguryu. Despite the frequent clashes, each state managed to hold its own. Matters came to a head in the seventh century when China challenged its most northern neighbor, Koguryu, sending in 300,000 troops. However, the Koguryuans lured the invading Chinese into an ambush on a scale never before seen. The warlike tribes of the Kogury kingdom put to the sword over 250,000 Chinese troops in a single day.

A few years later, before China could wreak her revenge upon Koguryu, the ruling dynasty ended and the T'ang dynasty was founded. Within the same year the king of Koguryu also

died, encouraging many to hope that a peaceful agreement between the two countries could be reached. Initially, all looked good as the three kingdoms sent peace envoys to the Chinese court. The Emperor Kao-tsu accepted their offerings and for a time peace did reign. However, it was not long before the three kingdoms were back at each other's throats, fighting skirmish after skirmish. With first one side winning, then the other, the T'ang emperor watched with interest, intending to form an alliance with the eventual winner. But there was then no way of knowing which kingdom would emerge triumphant.

Of the three kings Chim-p'yung of Silla was the most peace-loving and philosophical. He had a daughter who was renowned for her wisdom and love for the people. When her father died she ascended the throne, the first woman to rule a Korean kingdom, and dedicated herself to improving the living standards of her people. By now, neighboring Pak-je had fallen from favor with the Chinese rulers because it had been dishonest with the Emperor. The third warring kingdom, Kogu-ryu, had by now got a bloodthirsty queen on the throne.

China's Kao-tsu's problem was which ruler to side with. He knew that Queen Song-duk of Silla ruled with kindness and insight, rather than by the sword. But if he helped her fight the other two kingdoms he would have to provide her with a large army to support her small fighting force. But while Kao-tsu was struggling with his dilemma, the Queen Song-duk made up his mind for him. She impressed the Emperor by sending her best young warriors to Kao-tsu for training in the martial arts. She had instructed the warriors to be eager and willing to learn, but at the same time be humble and show great respect for the Chinese Emperor. Kao-tsu was very impressed with the Queen's approach, particularly when she later established her own martial arts' school where the soldiers trained the general public. Song-duk even drew up a special code of ethics to combine honesty, bravery, loyalty and justice with martial skills so that her young warriors would be more than just fighting machines. This code was called the *hwarang-do* (way of the flowering manhood). The Queen named this weaponless martial art after the Emperor of China, who had taught it to her soldiers. The name given was *T'ang-Shou*, meaning tang hand (from the Chinese T'ang dynasty).

In AD 644 the Emperor sent messengers to the other kingdoms, ordering them to cease attacking Silla unless they wanted to tackle the might of the Chinese army. From now on Silla, backed by the Chinese, blossomed and emerged as the strongest of the three kingdoms. And within 20 years all the lands of the Korean peninsula were united under the Silla flag. So the seeds that became the martial art of taekwondo were born.

Originally the hwarang was a code of ethics injected into a martial system. These young Korean warriors have often been likened to the Japanese samurai. The martial arts of t'ang merged with the ancient tae kyon, and soon its influence spread throughout the whole peninsula. As it was taught to soldiers, it was only natural that they would learn the weapon arts while also acquiring battlefield skills such as archery and sword and spear fighting. For nearly 300 years the population trained in martial arts at every level. The unarmed hand and foot techniques were almost elevated into a national sport, with even the farmers being ardent practitioners. There was not a village fête or town fair without at least one competition of hwarang-do fighters.

In AD 953 the kingdom of Silla was overthrown, and the Koryo dynasty was founded by Wang Kyon (the Koryo dynasty gave Korea the name by which it is known today). All martial arts were actively encouraged because the peninsula's survival was dependent on the existence of a strong army. But the Yi dynasty of 1392 so disliked the warring arts that it promptly disbanded the hwarang.

A few dedicated practitioners disappeared into the wild mountainous regions of Korea to practice their art in secret in the Buddhist monasteries. It was here that master and disciple preserved the true martial art of hwarang-do, passing it down from one generation to another, each adding its own refinements. It was not until the end of World War II that the martial art of hwarang-do emerged into the light of day, preserved and as effective as it had been almost 800 years previously.

The Korean systems became known by various names: *tang shu, soo bahk, kwonpup,* and its indigenous art *tae kyon.* Although many similarities exist between these forms they are not essentially the same.

Because the Yi dynasty banned all forms of martial art the unarmed combat systems either disappeared into the Buddhist temples or were

taken into central Korea, where they were practiced in relative secrecy. This move had a two-fold effect. First it split a systematized martial art still further, as the local native element of fighting merged with T'ang Sgu taking on a distinctively Korean characteristic. And second, the Chinese influence decreased. So the arts that were to unite under the flag of taekwondo, flourished for the next 500 years.

The next significant event came when Japan embarked on her course of Imperial

Left: *The incredible dexterity needed to perform high kicks is achieved by a gruelling series of leg stretching exercises. Here US patterns champion John Chung typifies the amazing control which comes from hard work and dedication to martial training. A kick such as this requires the practitioner to have supple ham strings and a tremendous sense of balance.*
Right: *A 5th dan taekwondo master delivers a simple front kick to a young student's nose. The kick shows incredible control on the part of this Korean master.*

expansionism and invaded Korea in 1907. All existing martial arts were banned in an attempt to dampen the tremendously strong Korean military spirit. This existed until 1945, and the defeat of the Japanese nation.

After World War II Korea began to rebuild, which meant that the martial arts suddenly flourished again. The various martial disciplines were represented by five major schools – the *mooduk kwan, changmu kwan, jido kwan, kang duk kwan* and the *chungdo kwan*. The heads of these organizations met to form a unified association for the promotion of the martial arts.

Progress was cut short, however, by the start of the Korean War in 1950. During the three years of turmoil the influx of United Nations' forces brought the Korean martial systems to the attention of the Western world. American soldiers stationed in Seoul, however, had discovered Japanese karate five years previously when they had occupied Japan. Originally they had called this art 'Korean karate,' but now altered it to the Japanese pronunciation of kempo.

The Korean war brought a soldier called Choi Hong Hi into prominence. Choi taught the old system of *tae kyon* to his troops and was later promoted to general, becoming a prominent force in the promotion of the Korean martial arts. He developed a style called *chang hun*. After the war he suggested that the old Korean systems be united under the new name of *taekwondo*. Major changes were now taking place within the art. And when the US servicemen returned home they found that these Asian martial arts were very popular with the general public. The soldiers who had gained black belts during their stay in Korea now opened up academies to teach this new art.

The Western influence quickly made an impact on the arts by gearing them to sporting competitions, although the new instructors did rely on the Koreans for guidance in organizing and regulating their tournaments. Some of the old masters, however, refused to help, not wanting to see their ancient martial heritage turned into a combat sport, with new rules and regulations.

The new group of masters that wished to retain and preserve the martial character of tae kyon broke away from the mainstream to go it alone. Meanwhile, the first competitive championships were staged in 1956 and, within a

Above: *In order to test the strength and impact of a good kick, students of taekwondo train on special foam pads.*
Left: *The flying kick has many advantages. It enables a smaller person to retaliate against a much taller attacker by suddenly leaping up into the air and kicking once the right height has been attained.*
Right: *One of the most difficult flying kicks to perform is the jumping sidekick.*

few years, taekwondo gained government recognition as a national sport. In 1972 the World Taekwondo Federation was founded and based its headquarters at the Kukkiwon in Seoul, overseeing more than 100 million people who practice the art. By far the biggest following in the Western world is in the United States, which accounts for more than 75 percent taekwondo practitioners.

Taekwondo has become a dramatic way for promoting Korean culture around the world. It evolved from a disciplinary exercise practiced by a small band of determined warriors to a sophisticated, modern-day means of self-protection.

Taekwondo, like all the martial arts, is much more than a mere fighting system. Its training program encompasses both physical and mental disciplines to improve the student's body and character. *Taekwondo-ists* (practitioners of the art) are quickly informed that the art was developed as a defense against enemy attacks and that it is not only geared to improving health and physical fitness, but also embraces a philosophy of self-discipline. Consequently, beginners are always instructed to adopt the 'correct attitude.'

The place of training is termed a *dojang*. Students train in white cotton uniforms and bare feet on a matted or wooden floor. The uniform (*tobok* or *dobock*) consists of trousers and either a wrapover jacket or vee-neck shirt, depending on the style practiced. The uniform is completed by a colored belt of rank *(kup)* worn over the top. Training usually begins with the students practicing in lines, getting to grips with the basic technique. Then they progress to combination movements and to free sparring with partners. All these techniques are practiced with extreme caution. The free sparring develops co-ordination and quick reflexes.

As a student progresses, he or she will learn how to execute and apply particular techniques, eventually aiming to adapt these movements to suit his or her own needs and build and to take part in competitions. It is important that the taekwondo-ist develops an individual fighting style and strategy to give him or her an edge over rivals, all of whom would have been taught exactly the same basic principles. This encouragement to cultivate individual styles ensures that in competitions no two competitors will fight using exactly the same techniques.

Competitions are fought (unlike in karate) with contestants wearing body armor. This consists of a padded breastplate fastened at the rear, padded hand mitts or gloves, and a special soleless shoe made from foam-like polystyrene. Full-contact kicks and punches are delivered to specific target areas on the body, each of which are worth a certain number of points. Fights are limited to a predetermined number of rounds and the person scoring the most points in the allotted time is the winner. The competitors must conduct themselves properly, displaying a good fighting spirit, the highest standard of technical ability, and strictly observe the rules of etiquette to the judges, referees, and to the opponent.

Taekwondo is unique on account of its kicking technique, which, to an extent, is the hallmark of the taekwondo-ist. A high degree of technical brilliance is vital if the kick is to become an explosive weapon and, when used correctly and competently, can be as accurate as hand-strikes and punches. The main advantage of the kicking technique is that you can attack or counterattack from further away, and generate two to three times more power force. If your opponent is moving in to attack you at the moment of impact, the force of the kick will be even greater. The main value of knowing how to use your feet is that you can practically double your means of self-protection.

Since taekwondo is based on a philosophy of non-violence it discourages the use of weapons. However, it does permit the use of the body's natural weapons, particularly the hands and feet. But since the legs are the body's most powerful natural weapon they receive special attention in training.

The trained taekwondo-ist has a devastating array of spectacular kicks. Experts can launch themselves off the ground to gain extra height before delivering an airborne attack with the legs. Some exponents can even strike with a series of two or three kicks while still in the air, revealing the terrific speed with which these kicking techniques are executed. The element that increases the kick's lethal potential is what taekwondo-ists call *explosive power*. Explosive power is the ability to generate, at a moment's notice, a co-ordinated, total effort to achieve a single goal. But this ability has to be developed, the basic techniques need to be practiced again and again, and only perseverance and hard work will lead to success.

Above: *During taekwondo competitions all contestants wear protective equipment including a padded body vest and a groin box. Here a contestant delivers a superb roundhouse kick.*

In the early stages of learning the art a new student learns the 119 vital body points, and how to keep them protected at all times. He or she will also have to cope with instructions being given in Korean. Because of the deep moral theme underlying taekwondo, everyone has to obey the five *jeong-sin* (tenets) of taekwondo – which are etiquette, modesty, perseverance, self-control and indomitable spirit.

No matter which martial art one has chosen to study, forms or patterns are an important part of training. In taekwondo these type of kata movements are known as *poomse* or *hyung*. Practicing a hyung involves using potentially dangerous techniques but only against an imaginary opponent. The hyung is the means of binding the basic techniques together and creating a fluid movement. When the beginner advances to the more ambitious techniques of taekwondo, he learns a *hyung* (pattern) which is a blueprint for linking these movements together. There are hyungs of varying degrees of difficulty at all levels which ultimately lead to a complete mastery of the technique.

Repetition is the key to gaining maximum potential from the hyungs. Constant practice with the same pattern day after day eventually enables the taekwondo-ist to perform the hyung almost automatically. This ability to use a variety of complicated techniques, without having to think about them, creates a state of mind where the practitioner can react to danger instinctively and immediately with a counter or block.

Above: *A taekwondo tournament at the 1986 Asian games. Note that the fighters are wearing headguards as well as body armor.*

Left: *Like the other martial arts, taekwondo is very strong on etiquette and discipline. Here two competitors bow to each other before the fight begins.*

Right: *A German competitor is blocked as he delivers a roundhouse kick. In competition head kicks score three points.*

The first pattern that is learned in taekwondo is the *taegeuk poomse*. Poomse means pattern or form, and taegeuk the origin of all things in the universe (it derives from tae, meaning bigness, and geuk, meaning eternity). This is a simple pattern, and has only 18 movements. The rudiments of knitting together the first basic techniques are portrayed in this first form.

The practitioner is made to realize that he is fighting an unseen adversary. He must differentiate between offensive and defensive moves and know their specific retaliatory purpose. In addition, the student must target and focus his strikes, instead of just randomly punching his unseen opponent. Every movement in the pattern has to be performed with the correct breathing techniques. The student has to learn how to co-ordinate his breathing or become short of breath. Practicing the patterns requires close attention to detail if the correct results are to be achieved. For instance, when delivering a strike the student exhales as he delivers the punch, so creating a blow with 20 percent extra power. At the same time he emits a *ki-yup* (shout or scream) similar to the karate kiai.

When a student is practicing by himself the hyung becomes his instructor, helping him flow through movement after movement, mentally and physically correcting him in the search for a flawless technique.

A properly executed power shout, or ki-yup, gives the practitioner a great psychological advantage. It not only intimidates an aggressor, but the unexpected war-cry gives the taekwondo-ist an invaluable split second to strike while his attacker is momentarily taken aback. In effect, it gives the practitioner a vital edge, an edge that can mean all the difference between success and failure.

It is often said that the hands and feet are the foundation of a good martial artist. This is particularly true of taekwondo, whereas Western boxers, for example, or even kung fu practitioners, elevate hand techniques above all else. A taekwondo-ist without a kick is like a revolver without bullets. Furthermore, most of the world's full and semi-contact champions have at one time practiced taekwondo.

Super-power kicks for combat do not come easily even through basic training. They have to be worked at through a series of physically demanding stretching exercises. The key to success is extremely supple legs, without which the dynamic execution of kicks will never be attained. Flexibility training, therefore, has to go hand-in-hand with the development of muscle strength and taekwondo-ists take this area of training to the absolute limit. They have no choice – the kick is their most important weapon. One of the world's finest taekwondo masters, who has developed his stretching and kicking abilities to their fullest potential, is the US-based master Hee Il Cho, an eighth dan. Master Cho shot to fame many years ago after displaying his amazing versatility with flying kicks and turning kicks and since then has become one of the leading figures in world taekwondo circles whom students everywhere strive to emulate.

Most beginners regard stretching, like the hyung, as a chore. But it is a very necessary chore, for the student who does not practice wholeheartedly loses out to badly executed and ineffective techniques. Furthermore, stretching exercises are essential for avoiding injuries. The taekwondo practitioner puts such stress on the knee joints, ankles, groin and hamstrings that strains are always likely. And since there is also the danger that he or she will get too carried away and use his or her other leg in wholly unnatural ways, constant supervision by an instructor is also a good idea.

The taekwondo practitioner aims for supple legs because they provide speed, and speed increases the force of the impact. But when undertaking a stretching program certain rules have to be observed to ensure that it is done properly and safely. For instance, muscles should always be given a chance to stretch of their own accord. You should never push, jolt, bounce or move sharply because this exerts undue tension on the delicate muscle structures. Every action must be carried out smoothly, without force. And finally, stretching should never be practiced until you have warmed up with preliminary exercise. So, the popular idea that jumping out of bed first thing in the morning to perform 'the daily dozen' is good for you does not hold true for taekwondo stretching. This is because lying in bed will have already stretched the spine, and gruelling stretching exercises early in the day merely exert unnecessary stress on the body. The ideal time is therefore around midday or early evening. In fact stretching exercises early in the evening can be positively therapeutic; they aid relaxation and improve the circulation.

Since there are many parallels between

Below: *One of the greatest taekwondo practitioners of all time, Master Hee Il Cho. He now teaches taekwondo in the United States.*
Right: *This Korean master's incredible ten-foot leap in the air culminates in him smashing his foot through a two-inch-thick piece of pine. Taekwondo experts smash all manner of materials with their hands and feet, perfecting their 'destruction techniques.'*

taekwondo and karate, it is not surprising to find that this Korean art also has power-breaking methods, or destruction techniques. The purpose of these breaking techniques is not to impress people by the extent to which flesh and bone can smash through concrete, but to instill into the practitioner the real power he or she can possess through correct training methods. Because of this, destruction tests are part of the grading syllabus, but the taekwondo student does not acquire his breaking power by application of brute force but through a training program informed by scientific, physical and mental principles.

When the student has cultivated a special kind of strength, far removed from simple brute force, he can then, for example, smash blocks of concrete or slice through piles of

Above: *This taekwondo blackbelt has executed a front flying kick from a near-standing position, a very difficult maneuver.* **Left:** *Karen Shepherd demonstrates the power that can be generated with the flying-kick technique. The last ten years have seen many more women participate in taekwondo.*

roofing tiles. This strength comes from within. Some schools, particularly those in Korea, encourage their students to build up callouses on the hand as a form of protection, but it is not essential. When the fully prepared taekwondoist wants to engage in power-breaking, there is little else to do other than concentrate, approach the object, and finally smash it in two.

If a student is to attain such levels of expertise in breaking he must first learn the six basic rules, which are confidence, concentration, technique, equilibrium, breath control and focus. The student must have confidence in his or her capabilities, believing without letting in any self-doubt, that he or she can destroy the materials. There is a great difference between saying and believing you can break an object. Nor should the student become cocky and overconfident, which is as bad as self-doubt. Being ready to test the power of technique against solid objects is very much a personal feeling. The student knows if he is ready or not.

The next step is concentration – the student must clear his mind of everyday events and thoughts, and concentrate solely upon focusing his power on the task at hand. The disciplined mind will eliminate all distractions. At this stage it is not unreasonable for the student to experience a slight ripple of fear, but fear is the ultimate distraction and has to be conquered before progressing with the break.

But what is involved in the actual breaking technique? Students can select either the head, shin, foot, fist or elbow, after which they must adjust their body position. Balance at this stage is of the utmost importance – if their equilibrium is off, even slightly, then not only might the break fail but also students could damage themselves. Students must rehearse the movement of the breaking action several times before attempting the actual break. During this 'rehearsal time' the student corrects his breathing pattern. Regulating the breathing is an essential part of all the arts, not just for breaking, but also for attacking and defending. Controlled breathing can even improve technique – for example, exhaling at a critical moment can actually accelerate a blow.

Students who have learned and can properly execute the five basic rules will increase their power, speed and balance. Focus, the last of the requirements, involves applying and directing body energy at a specific instant to a specific target. This use of this force creates a lightning, destructive stroke that can only otherwise be seen in full combat. Once a student has performed his first successful break he or she will become increasingly aware of the awesome power at his or her command, and will be filled with self-confidence.

Anyone who becomes remotely involved with taekwondo cannot but help be aware of the surrounding political difficulties. The problem for the beginner is which of the two major world associations, the World Taekwondo Federation (WTF) and International Taekwondo Federation (ITF) he should join. In 1961 all the old groups of Korean martial arts united under the banner of the Korean Taekwondo Association, with General Choi as its first president. Choi then founded ITF to spread the art around the world and, as its first ambassador, gave demonstrations in many foreign countries. Choi even went to communist-governed North Korea. However, this non-political trip stirred up a lot of trouble with his own government in South Korea. His

supporters turned against him and he was under political pressure to stand down as president and relinquish his honorary ninth dan ranking. The row split the Korean Taekwondo Association down the middle, although General Choi refused to give up the presidency, he thought it prudent to leave the country and settled, with the ITF, in Canada.

Meanwhile the KTA elected a new president, Yung-Wun Kim who, in 1973, created a new international governing body called the World Taekwondo Federation. This new body quickly set about creating its own distinct style of taekwondo to distinguish it from Choi's.

Today, these two international organizations look after about 80 percent of taekwondo, but when the WTF established its own identity, it also sacrificed a few important elements of the art. Its tournament rules in particular caused some surprise. The ITF decided that a well-executed kick to an opponent's head can score maximum points, but that a first strike to the face results in instant disqualification. Yet of the two techniques, the kick is the most dangerous.

Despite the fact that Korea has suffered an enormous political turmoil in the past 50 years, suppressing its martial arts and then using them for political ends, taekwondo has survived. And there can be no doubt that the 2000-year-old art will continue to do so.

Another of the Korean martial arts is *hapkido* (way of the co-ordinated power). It is an art almost exclusively for self-defense. In hapkido there are no patterns or sporting links; the techniques are too dangerous to allow for that. The art is also unusual in that it emphasizes a non-violent code of counterdefense. For instance, in an attack a hapkido practitioner remains calm until his aggressor has made the initial advance and committed himself to a strike. The hapkidoist then applies a soft, circular block and deflects the blow. A series of counteroffensive techniques follows that usually result in the attacker being totally annihilated. The art combines the same principles found in aikido with the strong kicks and punches from the Korean taekyon.

The art of hapkido consists of three main skills: non-resistance when meeting force, circular motions in countering and attacking, and an idea called the water principle. The water principle involves the total penetration of an enemy's defense. It is usually likened to a stream of water flowing downhill which, on

Above: *Son of the grandmaster of hwarang-do, Henry Lee dispatches two attackers simultaneously with a drop-down whipping throw. Hwarang-do (the flowering manhood) dates back to ancient times in Korea. Apart from in Korea, this martial art is most widely practiced in the United States, where the current grandmaster is master Joo Bang Lee.*

encountering an object, flows on round it. Similarly, hapkido never defends an attack with a solid block but steps to the side to deflect the blow, directing the force of the attack around the body. The attack is, therefore, simultaneously accepted and neutralized in a circular motion. It is a subtle art which bears out the old adage, 'You are still learning hapkido until the day you die.'

The absence of patterns or sporting versions have meant that hapkido has not become a diluted art, like so many others, and that its techniques for self-defense are as effective as ever. Another advantage of the art is that since strength is not a prerequisite, it is excellent for women, particularly those wanting to learn self-defense.

One of the most important aspects of hapkido's fighting philosophy is the avoidance of the pre-set sparring forms, notably the kicking, punching and blocking methods often found in other martial arts' training. Hapkido impresses upon the practitioner the necessity of continuous flowing attacks and, when he or she is on the defensive, fast, flowing and rhythmic countermeasures that will stop and disable an opponent.

Hapkido does not have a very long history, although it does have links with Korea's *buldo mu sool* (Buddhist monks' martial arts). Its

modern resurgence was mainly due to Yong Shul Choi who, in 1910, went to Japan to study a martial art that was a blend of the old Japanese aiki jutsu and jujitsu, called *daito ryu aiki jutsu*. Choi did not return to Korea for nearly 40 years, until after World War II, when he introduced his hapkido to his homeland. Since it was difficult to master it was not initially well received, but a small group of stalwarts did eventually conquer its many techniques.

The development of hapkido on a world scale was largely due to the efforts of a Korean master named Bong Soo Han who, as an unarmed combat instructor in Vietnam, introduced the art to the US special service groups. Later he went to live in the United States where, as an ex-student of Choi, he was granted permission to open his own academy.

Apart from locks and leverage holds, hapkido employs a wide range of kicking techniques, many of which are almost acrobatic. But with little effort a student of this art can soon learn to execute mid-air kicks, striking with both feet at the same time.

Soo bahk do was renamed *tang soo do* by its modern founder, master Hwang Kee, though in Korea it is still known by its old name. In 1945 Hwang Kee founded the organization Moo Duk Kwan (Institute of Martial Virtue) to promote the study of tang soo do. However, it must be pointed out that Hwang Kee did not create tang soo do, he only renamed it (the name means T'ang Dynasty hand way).

Hwang Kee was born in an area of Korea now known as the demilitarized zone. In his youth he travelled to China to study their martial arts and, during these formative years, was exposed to many different styles and systems. Kee became a student of Chinese philosophy and classical writings and, in the late 1940s, returned to Korea to found an

Above, far left: *Some Korean arts employ joint locks and holds that are rather similar to jujitsu. These kuk sool won exponents are engaged in a headlock which culminates in a throw. After the headlock has been achieved (***above center***) the master then drops down on his legs and throws his partner into the air. After the assailant is thrown (***above***) it is usual for the thrower to maintain a hold on the area of the opponent's body from which he first threw him.* **Right:** *A tremendously powerful front kick lifts the opponent completely off his feet.*

establishment for the furtherance of martial arts. Tang soo do is a way of life for its practitioners (not a means of self-defense) who believe that the spiritual must be balanced with the physical life to create a harmony that leads to the perfect fighting technique.

The emphasis upon the kicking techniques in tang soo do sometimes leads observers to believe that it is a purely kicking art. The phrase 'self-improvement through the art' is its ultimate tenet and tournaments always ensure that the rulings and etiquette are correctly observed.

The beginner starts by learning the five basic hyung. Interestingly, these hyung bear a remarkable resemblance to the Japanese heian katas. And some schools of thought believe that tang soo do is, in part, a disguised form of Shotokan karate but involving the indigenous Korean high kicks.

In retrospect, the Korean martial arts are not as diversified as the Japanese and Chinese martial system. Korea was occupied by both China and Japan in its long history, and was influenced by both countries' fighting techniques. Even in modern times Korea has suffered much internal conflict. As a result Korea's indigenous martial arts never really developed and matured in their purest forms.

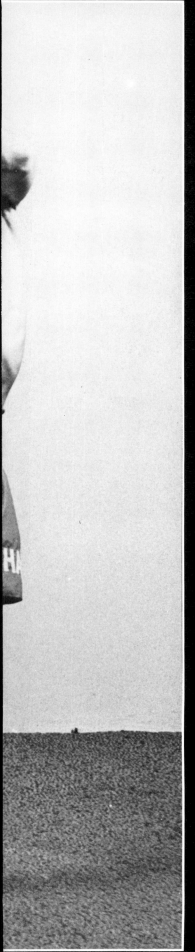

THE MARTIAL ARTS OF SOUTHEAST ASIA

Life unfolds on a great sheet called time, and once written is gone forever

Chai Sirisute, the top Thai
boxing exponent in the
United States, delivers a
low-point kick to his
opponent's thigh.

hand and a short dagger in the other, they were extremely ferocious warriors.

Under the Spanish influence the Moros were introduced to *escrima*. This is an art utilizing two hardwood sticks about 30 inches long. Escrima is also known under its Spanish name, *arnis de mano* (harness of the hand). Filipino twin-stick fighting, or escrima (meaning skirmish), is quite spectacular to see in action for the fighter's hands move so fast that they practically become a blur. There are many styles of stick fighting because each island developed its own particular method. The art of escrima is based upon a pattern of angles – the footwork moves along the lines of a triangle preventing the escrimador (one who trains in escrima) from being cornered.

Although kali, and its offshoot escrima, are always shown as either blade arts or stick arts it is really a complete martial art in itself. A master in the art is termed a *guru*. Traditionally, the old masters taught kali in 12 stages or categories, beginning with the long and short stick. However, twin knives can easily be substituted causing no problems since the technique remains the same. In addition kali argues that a fighter cannot go into combat with a predetermined idea of how he is going to react when attacking or on the defensive. The student has to be able to flow from one technique to another, retaining his effectiveness no matter what range he is fighting from. This does not mean that he has to be well versed in thousands of different techniques, merely that he must understand the principles of motion. Such understanding yields excellent results, for the only reason that kali has survived so long is that it is an extremely effective art.

The Moro natives of the Philippines were such superb fighters that they were never subdued, even when they had to contend with the Americans in 1898. The Moros, armed with bolos, harassed the US marines very successfully during the occupation. It seems quite amazing that invaders of these islands were always being shown up by the relatively unsophisticated natives using their indigenous martial art. The great explorer Ferdinand Magellan in 1521 landed on the island of Cebu, 700 miles south of Manila, and was met on the beach by Moros who were armed with double knives as dictated by their martial art of kali. The invaders had all the latest weaponry of the day, yet they still could not beat these fierce

The rich variety of martial arts that exist in Asia are a stepping stone for enthusiasts who wish to follow disciplines other than those of China or Japan. There is a huge variety, from the Philippines to India, from which to choose – all having one thing in common – they were born out of adversity.

The collection of tiny islands in the South China Sea are called the Philippines. Being on the main trading routes they came into constant contact with other nations, and absorbed different influences into their own technique called *kali* (knife or blade). The Muslim Filipinos, known as Moros, had once developed an ancient island system to produce a devastating martial system that did not necessarily require weapons. (Interestingly, unlike the other martial arts where the unarmed methods are learned first, in kali the weapons come first and the empty-hand techniques last.) The Moros used to fight with a knife called a *bolo* (similar to a machete), and with this weapon in one

Above, far left: *The kali practitioner armed with the deadly kris makes a frightening adversary.*

1. The attacker (right) strikes with a short stick. It is blocked and then countered by the defender cutting the hand with his knife.

2. The defender snakes his arm over the attacker's stick.

3. Snaking over then under and upward, the defender is halfway to trapping his attacker's weapon.

4. Sensing the impending danger the attacker quickly thrusts his dagger at the defender. Still using the snake motion, the defender snakes his hand around the attacker's dagger arm.

5. The defender then locks both the stick and the dagger of the attacker, so he is now trapped.

6. Finally the defender places his dagger at the throat of his attacker, to bring about a submission.

warriors. The ensuing battle resulted in the death of Magellan. Another example of kali prowess occurred in World War II when the Japanese invaded the Philippines. Many Filipinos joined the US forces but found great difficulty in using modern rifles and automatic weapons. After much petitioning and some incredible demonstrations by the Filipinos in the use of kali, the US army issued them with their favorite weapon, the bolo. From then until the end of the war these brave warriors waged a particularly vicious guerrilla campaign against the Japanese.

After World War II many Filipinos settled in southern California, around the Stockton area, merging their own kali into the American martial arts scene. One of the top contemporary American instructors of escrima is Dan Inosanto who, for a long time, lived with the late Bruce Lee when he came to America.

Kalaripayit (from *kalari* meaning battleground, and *payit* meaning training) is an martial art that has been practiced for nearly 2000 years in southern India, though until quite recently it was virtually unknown even

to many Indians. Kalaripayit shares the distinction, with the Chinese fighting systems, of being one of the oldest in the world. The heartland of kalaripayit is in Kerala province, where this martial art is part of daily life and the training system is virtually the same as when the art was established.

It is a very hard school of martial art that has no sporting activity as an offshoot. More than any other martial art, kalari has many formal greeting rituals which are performed before practice begins. Kalari is a very sophisticated fighting system that includes unarmed techniques, with students being taught how to defend themselves with their bare hands against weapons, and armed methods.

At the advanced stages of learning, students fight each other with weapons ranging from knives and swords to a special spring-sword made from long, thin strips of metal, which are unique to India. Locking techniques are also used in the system to immobilize an opponent and disarm him. However, it takes years of practice before these techniques can be applied effectively.

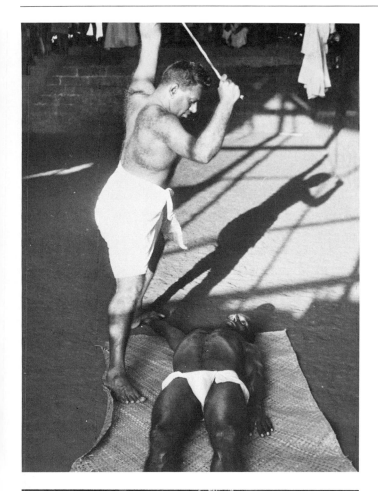

Above: *Two young women practicing self-defense with short sticks in the Indian art of selambam.*
Above left: *Kalaripayit students practicing barehand self-defense. Although very old, this Indian martial art has only recently come to light in the West.*

Top: *Students of kalari have to undergo a strict regimen of special massage treatment so that their bodies are fit to undertake the hard training involved. A master holds onto a cord to maintain his balance as he walks on the student's body, giving him a foot massage.*

In the martial arts there are many ways of striking an opponent with the hand or foot. Kalaripayit is unique in that it uses the feet to block incoming attacks. In addition, students are taught body maneuvering such as feinting and diving around the attacker, and beneath his kicks or punches.

Kalaripayit, like so many other martial arts systems, is much more than just a fighting art for it involves a detailed understanding of the human body. Since fighting inevitably leads to injury most masters of kalaripayit are also doctors. The medicine they practice is *Marma*, the traditional Indian system, which is a branch of the *ayurvedic* medicine, which involves both massage and herbal medicines.

There are actually two styles of kalaripayit, one practiced in the south mainly by the Tamil people, and one in the north about which less is known. This style is used by descendants of the Nayers, who were once a ferocious warrior caste. The northern style has incredibly high-kicking maneuvers and low scything, foot sweeps and is more deeply informed by religion than is the southern style. The northern style also involves deep-breathing exercises, based on yoga techniques.

The kalari is the place of practice and is the equivalent of a Japanese dojo. It measures exactly 21 feet by 42 feet (these measurements are vital if the rituals are to be properly observed). The uniform resembles the nappy type of garment worn by the sumo wrestlers of Japan, but incredibly measures 40 feet in length. A student puts on his costume by tying one end of it to a palm tree and the other end around his waist. Then in a series of twisting motions, he winds it round him so that it acts like a truss, protecting the groin and pelvic bone.

Both the styles have four main branches: unarmed training, *selambam* (a type of stick or pole fighting), weapon art (of the bladed variety), and finally a technique known as *marma-adi*. The latter is only taught to the most advanced students because it involves attacking the vital points of the body. All northern practice is conducted at night and in secret.

The art is very tough and rugged, with participants being thrown onto a solid stone floor. Consequently, the students have to be extremely supple and therefore practice stretching exercises regularly. One of the arts' strangest routines is the crocodile walk, which resembles a push up but which is executed

while walking up and down the floor. Kalaripayit fighters are also taught to execute blocks and attacks from an almost seated position. Crouching low on the ground, the practitioner performs amazing leaps into the air to heights of up to eight feet (this feat requires extremely strong legs). Landing back on the ground the kalari fighter can fall into a full drop splits with all his weight behind it.

The rituals of kalaripayit demand that all students are obedient and pay their respects to Kali, the goddess of war. Kali was reputedly responsible for the cult of thugee, an anti-British organization in the nineteenth century. Its devotees were bent on ridding India of imperialism and, to this end, strangled people, mostly British sympathizers, by means of a rupee (small Indian coin) encased within the folds of a silken scarf. The coin was placed against the victim's windpipe and crushed the larynx, resulting in death. The English word thug derives from this cult.

Kalaripayit is predominantly a village art and is rarely seen in the towns and cities of southern India. It was reportedly based on the *sastras*, secret esoteric writings passed down through the ages with instructions written on palm-leaf scrolls.

In the ancient kingdom of Siam (now Thailand), it was common to settle a dispute of national importance by a duel in unarmed combat. According to one story, in 1411 two princes had been waging war against each other for quite a time, neither gaining the upper hand. It was suggested that the issue be settled by a single-combat match. Each side had to choose a champion boxer, and they would fight until blood was drawn. Whoever lost this duel would forfeit his right to the throne. The match was said to have lasted over seven hours before one of the boxers scratched his foot and lost the fight when he bled.

Above, far left: *Thai boxing master about to deliver a sok, or flying-elbow technique.*
Above left: *A Thai classical dance relates the legend of Ravana and Hanuman the monkey god versus the demon.*

Left: *Thai boxing master Toddy generates internal energy as concrete blocks are smashed on his chest.*
Right: *Therevada Buddhist priests outside a temple in Bangkok, 1911. Most Thai boxers serve as novice monks for a short period. Prayers are offered to Buddha before each fight.*

Throughout Thai history, *muay thai*, to give the boxing art its correct name, has figured prominently. But, during the reign of Pra Chao Sua (who was known as 'the Tiger King') Thai boxing gained a new impetus because the king himself was not only an ardent fan of the art but was also a great boxing champion in his own right. He used to travel to village fairs incognito and fight local champions for prize money, without anyone ever realizing who he was. In fact, some of the present-day techniques in muay thai are said to have been based upon Pra Chao Sua's style of fighting.

In those days crude boxing gloves were fashioned out of hemp rope which had been soaked in glue. If ground glass was mixed into the glue, the results were devastating. An early type of groin guard took the shape of a clam shell; inland communities substituted the tree bark for the shell. But the sport was so violent that by the early twentieth century deaths in the ring were becoming frequent. Despite government intervention with rules which they hoped would reduce or entirely eliminate these fatalities, brain damage, deaths and serious injuries continued.

By 1930, however, modern boxing gloves, rules, regulations, weight divisions and fights staged in a modern ring made the art much safer. Muay thai had come of age. But it still was not entirely free of danger. Despite all the legislation deaths still occurred, mainly from the *sok* (elbow strike) to the temple.

Thai boxing is probably the toughest contact sport in the whole of the martial arts and its lethal techniques, delivered in swift succession, can penetrate even the best defenses. The West, however, was so wary of its reputation that the controlling powers eliminated the elbow strikes and other lethal characteristics to create the new, safer sport of kick boxing.

All muay thai training is geared toward first-rate fighting skills. New students are first taught footwork and leg movement because they dictate the range of the fighters's attack and defense. There are no real basic preliminaries in the art, just a series of short, set techniques that combine into a pattern for attack. An interesting aspect of the art is the use of the *yng kow* (long knee). This constitutes an all-in-one defense and attack. It can either be

aimed at an attack to the stomach or sternum, or converted from a knee strike into a front kick merely by extending the leg.

In Thai boxing, unlike other martial arts, the fighter learns to kick with his shin rather than other parts of the body. The shin is deliberately toughened up in training sessions by repeatedly pounding it against a heavy bag. Eventually, it has the force of an iron bar. Stamina training in muay thai is probably the most rigorous of any Asian fighting style. The students, who live in special boxing camps, jog for five miles at a time, followed up by a two- or three-mile swim. Without pausing for rest, the fighter then moves on to the punch bags for an hour's punching and kicking. Since fights can last a long time it is vital that the boxers are fit.

Below: *Thai boxing tournaments are held in boxing rings. Fighters are trained to kick with their shins rather than their feet.*

Right: *Lisa Howarth of England became the women's world Thai boxing champion, beating the Thai's at their own sport.*

Thai boxers are so superstitious that they enter the ring wearing a talisman, or good luck charm. It is concealed beneath a braid or cord, called a *kruang rang*, which is tied around the arm. And since the Thais are devout Therevada Buddhists they pray for victory before a fight and, if they are successful, pray again afterward to give thanks. Women are thought to bring bad luck to the sport, and at one time it was strictly forbidden for them to climb the steps to the ring, let alone get inside it. But times are changing and, in Bangkok, women's fights are now being promoted. Interestingly, Lisa Howarth from England recently learned the art of muay thai and then took on the Thai's national women's champion, beating her to take the world title.

Most westerners who have learned muay thai make the transition from Thai boxing to kick boxing in order to gain world titles in both sports. Lisa Howarth has become a champion in both sports.

Before a muay thai fight begins, there is a very important ritual to be observed called *ram muay*, a pre-fight ritual dance. No fighter would ever dream of competing in the ring without first practicing this dance which is accompanied by music from cymbals, drums, and jawa flutes. Since each training camp in Thailand has its own special dance routine it is possible to discern which camp a fighter comes from just by watching him perform this ritual.

The movements of the ram muay are executed with a slow, gyrating motion. Then the fighter salutes the audience and begins a series of gestures aimed at the opponent. Depending upon the camp he comes from he will hurl an imaginary spear, then assume that the missile killed the opponent, begin to dig a grave and finally bury his adversary. All of this is supposed to instill fear into the heart of the opponent (who also does his own dance) while building up the performer's confidence. When the dance is finished the fighter walks to his respective corner to bow his head in prayer before his teacher who then utters a short prayer for victory. Finally, he blows three times on the fighter's forehead. This is known as the Buddha breath.

Muay thai has rapidly spread through the West, and its popularity is still on the increase. This trend is probably a result of the West's active interest in contact sports.

Other lesser-known martial arts exist in and around Asia, such as the *bando* boxing system

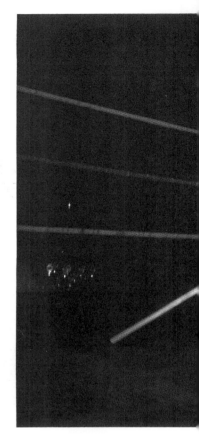

Right: *10th dan George Canning proves that, armed with a simple stick and the knowledge of how to best use it, one can defend oneself in any situation.*
Far right: *Bob Breen, instigator of the MCS or Modern Combat System (left), blocks a side kick with a rising-knee defense. The knee not only stops the attack but also destroys the muscle in the attacker's leg.*
Below: *One of the founders of the mugendo kickboxing system, Professor George Canning of Dublin (left), delivers a well-aimed roundhouse kick at his son George, who is a mugendo international kickboxing champion.*

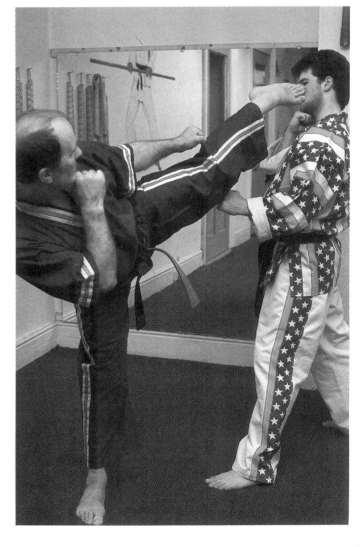

of Burma, which is based upon 12 animals. In Malaysia there is a hand and foot art known as *pentjak silat* which consists of many diverse forms. Russia has *sambo* wrestling, which developed in Oriental Russia. Each martial art offers not just a technique but a philosophy. Practitioners get out what they put in.

The changing face of the martial arts in recent years has led many students away from the traditional ways in search of something different. The tried and tested Oriental training methods have been re-examined by the logical Western mind in an effort to revamp certain areas of coaching. Consequently, the Japanese and Chinese hold over Western practice is fast in decline. In their place is an international style, which takes the best elements from a wide variety of sources in the search for the perfect martial arts system. This amalgamation of different styles, is termed 'eclectic.'

Some of these new systems have caught on in a big way and are very successful. Others have burst on the scene and then vanished quickly, without a trace. Bruce Lee's fighting method, jeet kune do, is an eclectic system that is enjoying a certain amount of success, although it takes up to 200 years before a system can be seen as an enduring style. Another style that seems to be taking off, especially in Europe, is that of *mugendo* (the

unlimited way). This martial art is a combination of karate kicking methods injected with the punches and footwork from Western boxing. All its main innovators are still alive and constantly improving the system, occasionally rejecting ineffective techniques and introducing new ones with more potential. Also, a competitive sporting form of mugendo has been introduced, with weight categories and, recently, world champions.

It seems certain that over the next 10 years or so many more eclectic styles will be introduced, each one purporting to outdo the other. Meanwhile, the future of self-defense techniques is guaranteed by urban violence, which will also be an important factor in shaping the new systems. But these systems differ in one very important respect from their ancient predecessors – they are devoid of any underlying philosophy or principles. One wonders how long the traditional Eastern martial arts would have lasted if they too had been nothing more than fighting techniques. Two thousand years ago these systems provided a vital answer to our quest for a life larger and more meaningful than one in which the fight for survival seemed to originate. They gave people broader horizons and higher ideals. The martial arts are not just about fighting, they are about living life to the full.

GLOSSARY

A double sai attack is countered by a double block.

ACUPUNCTURE Chinese system of medicine and healing, which uses needles on certain key points on the body. These points are known as meridians.

AIKIDO A Japanese martial art invented by Morehei Ueshiba. It involves internal and external harmony with nature. The techniques of this system are circular in movement. Other styles have been developed from the original founder's version.

ARNIS DE MANO Translated as harness of the hand, this Philippine martial art involves the use of twin sticks for fighting. It is also a dance in which the fighting art was disguised when the Spanish banned indigenous martial arts.

ATEMI Japanese art of attacking the vital points of the body. Used much in jujitsu, but illegal in judo contests.

BALISONG The correct term for the Filipino butterfly knife, first manufactured in the Philippines. It is a switchblade-type knife, that is opened by a downward wrist action. Much favored weapon of escrima and kali fighters.

BANDESH An Indian empty-hand fighting technique used to defeat an armed assailant, without actually killing him.

BANDO Burmese martial art involving numerous boxing methods. Based upon 12 animals, which are: the boar, bull, cobra, deer, eagle, monkey, bird, panther, python, scorpion, tiger and viper. Introduced into the West by Dr Mung Gyi in 1962.

BANSHAY Burmese form of weapon arts utilizing staff, sword and spear.

BERSILAT Martial art of Malaysia; derived from Indonesian pentjak-silat. Also practiced in Java and Sumatra.

BINOT An ancient form of weaponless fighting found in India. This art is reputed to be over 3000 years old. Binot means something to protect. The system is seldom practiced today.

BLACK BELT This belt represents the first significant rank in martial arts' training. When you have gained your black belt, you can then become a teacher. In the Japanese ranking system the black belt is known as shodan.

BO A six-and-a-half-foot staff, used by the Okinawans and Japanese in combat.

BODHIDHARMA The Indian holy man, also known as Ta'mo and Daruma, who is credited with bringing Zen Buddhism to China. This legendary figure introduced a series of exercises to the Shaolin Temple which is traditionally recognized as the basis for all Shaolin kung fu.

BOK HOK PAI A Chinese system of kung fu based on the mannerisms of the white crane.

BOKKEN A solid wooden sword used for training purposes in kendo and other martial arts. In the hands of an expert, this training weapon can deliver fatal blows.

BOK MEI PAI The very fast 'white eyebrow' style of kung fu, named after its founder Bok Mei. Legend states that it was banned at the Shaolin Temple because Bok Mei killed one of his fellow students in a fight.

BOXER REBELLION War against Western influence in China in 1900. It was so named by the Europeans because many of the Chinese fighters involved in the rebellion also belonged to a secret society called the I-Ho-Chuan, or Righteous and Harmonious Fists (consisting of many kung fu stylists from Chinese boxing).

BUDDHISM Eastern religion which spread from India to China, then to many parts of Asia. Buddha's real name was Siddartha Gautama (also called Sakyamuni). He was the son of an Indian king whose profound experience at the age of 28 led him to give up his rich lifestyle and adopt the mantle of a beggar.

BUSHI Means martial man, a Japanese term indicating a warrior who follows the code of bushido (way of the warrior). Bushido was the ethical code of the samurai which stressed honor, loyalty, duty and obedience.

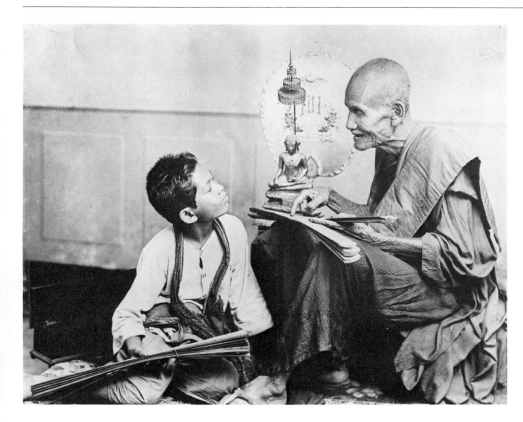

Above: *Thai priests at the turn of the century discuss Buddhism.*
Left: *A kung fu sifu adopts an attack pose with butterfly knives.*
Far left: *An aikido master executes a tremendous overhead throw.*

BUTTERFLY KNIFE A short, heavy, Chinese knife used in pairs. Proper name bot jum do. Popularly seen in the kung fu styles of wing chun and hung gar, but other styles have adopted it.

CAT STANCE A stance mainly used in some karate styles but also seen in kung fu. This stance places virtually all the body weight on the back leg, so that the practitioner resembles a cat about to pounce or spring.

CENTER LINE The basic theory of wing chun kung fu. Students are taught to defend and attack this imaginary line running down through the center of the body which is said to house all the vital organs.

CH'AN or CHAN The Chinese translation of Zen, it means meditation. In India it is known as Dhyana.

CHANG SAN-FENG The legendary martial art's master and great Taoist philosopher credited with founding tai chi chuan, one of the three internal systems of Chinese boxing.

CHANG-HON YU The school of taekwondo created by Choi Hong Hi. The name means blue cottage.

CH'IN-NA The Chinese art of seizing and grappling; it is a very sophisticated kind of wrestling. Practitioners cannot enter combat until they have acquired knowledge of anatomy, ensuring that they successfully apply the techniques of the system.

CHI Internal energy, the universal force which is harnessed through a series of special breathing exercises called chi kung, or gung. It brings its users good health and amazing physical strength. Its development is the prime requirement for practitioners of tai chi and hsing-i.

CHI SAO The special exercise in wing chun kung fu for developing co-ordination and sensitivity in the arms. It is also very important for teaching correct elbow positioning and economy of motion. Known in the West as sticking hands.

CHIEN or CHEN The oldest known style of tai chi chuan which has 108 postures. Originated in Chien village.

CHOY LI FUT Southern style of Chinese boxing based on the Shaolin Temple systems. Created in 1836 by Chan Heung.

CHUAN FA Chinese term meaning way of the fist. This is actually the correct terminology for what most people call kung fu.

CHUDAN In Japanese martial arts, the middle area or chest. In karate this is one of the three target points on the body.

CHUNGDAN The Korean term to indicate the mid-section of the body. Identified with Japanese chudan.

CHUNIN The middleman, one of the three ranks in ninjutsu.

CRANE One of the five animal styles of Shaolin kung fu.

DAN A Japanese term for anyone who has achieved the rank of black belt or above. This term is not exclusively applied to the martial arts but also to many other subjects, including swimming and the board game *go*.

DAISENSEI Great teacher, a title of respect given only to a teacher of very high rank.

DAITO Japanese long sword with a cutting edge measuring over 25 inches used by the samurai.

DAITO RYU A style of aiki jutsu from which it is said aikido developed.

DAISHO The matching set of Japanese long and short swords, worn by all samurai in the Tokugawa era.

DIM MAK The fabled death touch. A delayed-action strike aimed at an acupuncture meridian which can cause death to a victim within hours or even days after the blow has been delivered. Only a great master can deliver the death touch.

DIT DA JOW A special herbal and medicinal ointment, with a secret recipe. It is used to help prevent injury and severe bruising during training in almost all the Chinese martial arts.

DO Japanese word for path, or way. Used at the end of a name of a martial way such as karate-do or kendo.

DOJO Training place or hall, used for the practice of Japanese martial arts.

DOSHIN-SO The founder of the shorinji kempo martial art. It was greatly influenced by Chinese systems and is registered in Japan as a religious sect.

DRAGON One of the five animal styles practiced at Shaolin which teaches agility and flexibility. The mythical dragon symbolizes the spirit.

DRUNKEN MONKEY A style of kung fu based on the behavior of monkeys. Practitioners stagger around as though intoxicated, to fool an opponent into making a wrong move. This style employs many ground and low techniques.

ELBOW A close-quarter technique used in almost all martial systems. It is of particular interest to the muay thai fighters of Thailand.

EMPTY HAND The literal translation of the Japanese word karate.

ESCRIMA or ESKRIMA A martial system of the Philippines that employs sticks, swords and daggers. This is a Spanish term meaning skirmish.

FIVE ANCESTORS The five survivors who escaped during the sacking of the Shaolin Temple. They are credited with being the founders of the triad societies.

FIVE ANIMALS The movements of the crane, dragon, leopard, tiger and snake which inspired the Shaolin systems.

FORM A series of choreographed movements linking together various martial arts techniques. These techniques can be performed as a solo. Also known as kata or patterns.

FU HSING The Chinese god of happiness.

FU JOW PAI The tiger-claw system of kung fu. Developed at the Shaolin Temple.

FULL CONTACT A form of karate in which full-power kicks are delivered at an opponent. Participants wear protective hand and foot equipment. The sport has grown at an amazingly rapid rate in Western countries in the last 10 years.

GEDAN Area of the body from the waist downward in Japanese martial arts.

GENIN The lowest of the three ranks in the ninja hierarchy. The genin were the field agents or ninja who carried out assassinations.

GI The term used for the training uniform in Japanese martial arts. It is known as a karate-gi in karate, and a judo-gi in judo.

GICHIN FUNAKOSHI The founder of shotokan karate. An Okinawan schoolmaster, he is credited with introducing karate to Japan in 1922.

GOJU RYU One of the major styles of karate developed from Okinawan naha te. It is a hard-soft system invented by Chojun Miyagi.

GOJU KAI An offshoot of gojuryu karate; its founder was a student of Miyagi's named Gogen Yamaguchi and is nicknamed 'the cat.'

GULAT A type of wrestling found in Java, greatly influenced by sumo wrestling.

GUNG FU Cantonese pronunciation of kung fu.

GURU The term for a teacher in many martial arts systems. Of Muslim or Indian origin.

GYOJI The referee at a sumo wrestling match.

HACHIDAN An 8th-degree black belt (hachi means eight). In Japanese martial arts the title denotes a professor of the art.

HADAN The taekwondo term for the area of the body below the waist, equivalent to the Japanese geden.

HAKAMA Means divided skirt. It is a long skirt-type garment covering the legs and feet. Used in kendo and aikido and other Japanese martial arts. The long robe is said to mask the intricate footwork of the practitioner, therefore making it difficult for an opponent to judge his movements.

HAPKIDO A Korean martial art involving many difficult kicks, but also utilizing locks and holds. It is not too dissimilar from Japanese aikido.

HARA KIRI Japanese ritual suicide by disembowlment. Known in Japan by its proper term of seppuku. It was the ultimate act of atonement for the ancient samurai warrior who had lost honor or respect.

HARIMAU The tiger style of pentjak-silat of Indonesia.

HEIAN The name given to the five basic karate katas. In some schools the heian katas are also known as pinan katas.

HOJO-JUTSU The Japanese art of binding or rope tying. Adepts learn intricate methods of tying up a person with cord. Hojo-jutsu was first practiced by the samurai for detaining prisoners for questioning.

HO JUTSU The samurai art of using firearms.

HOP GAR A style of kung fu which became prominent during the Ching dynasty in China. It was famous as being the official martial art of the Manchu emperors and his guards. There are two distinct styles within the system – the white crane and law-horn. This style is also known by the name lama kung fu.

HORSE STANCE Or horse-riding stance; a popular basic stance in many Oriental martial arts, especially Chinese hung gar and Japanese karate (which refers to it as kiba dachi).

HSING I One of the internal systems of Chinese martial arts. Created by the great warrior Yueh Fei. This art is sometimes referred to as mind form boxing. The system is based upon the five elements.

HUANG TI The real name of the legendary Yellow Emperor of the Chou dynasty. He was thought to be the author of the *Nei-Ching*, the great Taoist classic on internal medicine.

HUNG GAR A popular style of kung fu stressing powerful hand techniques delivered from low stances. Hung gar is based upon the movements of the tiger and the crane and is one of the original five-ancestor styles. Hung is the creator's name, and gar means family or system.

HWARANG DO Means way of the flowering manhood. It is a combined code of ethics and a fighting system used by the Japanese samurai. This art was also practiced in the Silla kingdom of Korea. Today its main propagator in the West is grandmaster Joo Bang Lee who lives in the United States.

HYUNG The practice of patterns or forms, identified with the Japanese kata, used in taekewondo.

IAI DO Japanese martial way of drawing and resheathing a sword. It is a non-combat art geared toward intellectual and spiritual awareness.

IAI JUTSU The martial system from which iaido derives. This battlefield art involves the practitioner rapidly drawing his sword to kill an opponent, and then replacing it in its scabbard.

I CHING The great *Book of Changes*, an ancient book of Taoist divination principles. It provides the philosophical basis of tai chi chuan, pa kua, and hsing i. The treatise contains 64 six-line symbols or hexagrams, each composed of two, three-line symbols called trigrams. These symbols represent everything that exists in the universe.

IGA The remote and mountainous area in Japan where the ninja clans lived and trained.

IRON PALM A lethal kung fu technique which can kill with a single blow. The entire forearm (including the hand) must be conditioned for several years until it is as hard as an iron bar.

Above: *A jujitsu grip has stopped a punch from finding its target.*
Below left: *Soke Inoue uses the bo staff against a wooden kendo sword.*

JEET KUNE DO The style of kung fu formulated by the late Bruce Lee. The name means way of the intercepting fist.

JKA Japan Karate Association. Founded in 1955, is the largest karate association. Its first chief instructor was the founder of shotokan, Gichin Funakoshi.

JODAN The term used in Japanese martial arts to denote the top part of the body, above the shoulders.

JONIN The highest ninja rank.

JUDO Modern sporting form of jujitsu. Developed by Dr Jigoro Kano in 1882 and, to date, the only Oriental martial art performed in the Olympic Games.

JUDOKA One who practices judo.

JU JITSU A Japanese martial art in which the opponent's strength is turned against him. The art contains both armed and unarmed techniques. The term means soft or flexible.

JUKEN DO The way of the bayonet, a Japanese martial way that has recently adopted a sporting format. Involves fighting with a bayonet fixed to the end of a rifle. Juken do developed from spear and staff arts.

JUTSO or JITSU Japanese word meaning skill or art.

JUTTE or JITTE A single tined iron truncheon used by the early Japanese police force. The single tine at the hilt of the weapon enables the user to trap a katana (sword) without being injured by the blade.

KAMA An early Asian agricultural implement, similar to a sickle. It was used on the island of Okinawa as a weapon. Today, wooden kama are used in practice karate sessions and other Japanese martial arts as training devices.

KARATE or KARATE DO The way of the empty hand. A Japanese martial art employing kicks and strikes delivered to all areas of the body. Developed largely on Okinawa, it owes much to the Chinese systems of combat.

KARATE KA One who practices karate.

KATA A fixed series of movements in which the martial artist defends himself or herself against imaginary opponents. Kata are considered by many of the founding masters of karate to be the 'soul of the art.'

KALARIPAYIT An Indian system of martial training consisting of two styles, the northern and southern. Mainly dominated by the Tamils in the south and the descendants of the Nayar warriors in the north. The word means battlefield training.

KALI A martial art practiced in the Philippines. It involves learning 12 categories of disciplines. Beginners progress from weapons to the empty-hand methods. Kali practitioners claim that this is a complete martial system.

KATANA A Japanese sword.

KEMPO Japanese pronunciation of ch'uan fa, which is Chinese for way of the fist. It is a form of karate based upon Chinese systems and Korean taekwondo, using high-speed blocks and counterattacks, plus spectacular kicking methods. Kempo is very popular in the United States.

KENDO Modern Japanese fencing based upon the ancient warrior skill of kenjutsu. For safety reasons in the sporting form the live blade is substituted for a bamboo equivalent.

KI The Japanese translation of the Chinese chi, the vital energy within the human body. Development of ki is an important part of martial arts such as aikido and hapkido.

Above: *Sensei Katsutaka Tanaka with two wooden kammas.*

KIAI The loud shout or yell in Japanese martial arts. It accompanies an attacking move and both adds extra power and stuns opponents.

KIHON The basic training moves.

KOBUDO The ancient martial ways of Japanese warriors.

KRABI KRABBONG The armed, twin-sworded combat system of Thailand. Practitioners fight at lightning speeds using two, razor-sharp short swords or a sword and shield.

KUP One of the eight grades in taekwondo, comparable to the Japanese kyu grade.

KUSARIGAMA A weapon consisting of a sickle attached by a long chain to a weighted end. It was used for trapping and ensnaring victims, and was highly regarded by the ninja.

KYOKUSHINKAI A Japanese karate system, meaning way of ultimate truth, founded by the Korean-born Masatatsu Oyama. Oyama gained fame by fighting bulls barehanded. He still holds the world record for breaking the greatest number of roofing tiles with one blow.

KYUDO Way of the bow; the Japanese martial art of archery informed by Zen. Great emphasis is attached to the practitioner's attitude and to the way in which he or she fires the arrow. Hitting the target is of little consequence.

LAO TSU Legendary sage in Chinese history credited with founding Taoism. Author of the great taoist philosophic work, the *Tao Te Ching*.

LATHI or LATHE The Indian art of fighting with a staff.

LO HAN Name of any famous disciple of Buddha. Also the name of the exercises that Bodhidharma taught to the monks at Shaolin when he found them in an emaciated condition. The method of training, known as the 18 hands of the lo han, the basis of what we now call kung fu.

LUNG The Chinese word meaning dragon.

MABUNI KENWA Kenwa Mabuni was the creator of Shitoryu karate. Like Funakoshi he studied under Itosu while on Okinawa.

MARTIAL ARTS The term denoting the arts of war, taken from mars, the god of war. Now means a fighting discipline to promote combat proficiency.

MEN The name given to the face mask or helmet used in kendo.

MOON JOONG Wooden dummy, shaped like a man and used for conditioning and training, in many hard or external styles of kung fu (notably wing chun and hung gar, and kuen).

MOO DUK KWAN A Korean term for the academy for martial practice.

MAKIWARA A striking post used for conditioning the hands and feet in karate.

MUAY THAI Correct term for Thai boxing.

NAGINATA A Japanese halbard or curved, bladed spear. Used in the martial art of naginata do. This art was adopted by women and is now a thriving combat sport in Japan, with the spear tip having been replaced with a piece of bamboo for safety.

NAHA TE One of the three original styles of Okinawan karate, named after the town of Naha where it was first practiced.

NINJA Secret society of highly trained assassins in Japan. They were trained from birth as experts in a vast number of martial skills. Ninja literally means stealers in.

PATTERN See form or kata.

PRAYING MANTIS Known in China as tong long. Praying mantis is a kung fu style named after Wong Long who invented the style having witnessed a fight between a grasshopper and a praying mantis.

RANDORI Free practice or sparring in judo, where techniques are not pre-arranged.

ROKUSHAKUBO Okinawan six-foot staff or pole made from oak, or similar hardwood. Roku means six, shaku is a measure about a foot long, and bo is a pole or staff.

Above: *The ninja's kusarigama.*
Top: *Bruce Lee with nunchaku.*

NINJUTSU The art or techniques of the ninja. Their name was originally shinobi.

NUNCHAKU Two wooden batons linked by a short chain or cord turning it into an awesome weapon. Used orginally as a rice flail, this weapon can be found throughout Asia.

OKINAWA TE The collective term for the schools of Okinawan karate. The name means Okinawa hand.

PA KUA Internal style of kung fu, based on circular movements with open-palm strikes. The concept comes from the Chinese classic the *I Ching*, or *Book of Changes*. This art involves continuous changes of direction during an attack. Consequently the art is sometimes known as eight-direction palm boxing.

PENTJAK SILAT Indonesian martial art of muslim and Chinese origin. There are many hundreds of different styles.

ROUNDHOUSE KICK Kick used in virtually all the martial arts. Its circular path gives it extra power from centrifugal force. It is probably one of the most powerful kicks in the martial artist's arsenal.

RYU In Japanese martial arts it means school or style.

SAI Three-pronged fork-like weapon once made of iron, now of steel. It resembles a short, blunt sword. The sai was an effective weapon against an attack by sword or bo (staff). It is a single-handed weapon used in pairs.

SAMURAI Japanese feudal warrior (the word means one who serves), often likened to the medieval knights of Europe. A samurai served as a military retainer to the lords and shogun. The word samurai replaced the old word bushi (warrior). A masterless samurai was known as a ronin.

SANCHIN A breathing exercise of 20 movements used in Okinawan karate. Sanchin teaches practitioners how to tense the body and control breathing during intense combat.

SAVATE Or, more correctly, *la savate*. French system of foot fighting which was the forerunner of traditional French boxing – *la boxe française* – used in Paris by the underworld. Influenced by Chinese martial arts.

SENSEI Japanese word meaning teacher or instructor.

SIKARAN Found on the Philippine island of Luzon, sikaran stresses kicks and leg techniques. It resembles some Japanese systems of martial arts.

SHAOLIN The temple in the Songshan Mountains of Northern China, where it is alleged kung fu was born.

SHIAI In kendo, a match or contest in which two kendoka use a veriety of techniques to try to score points.

SHINAI Bamboo sword made of four strips bound together. Used in kendo to replace the live blade.

SHINOBI The old term, from which the name ninja derives; it means stealers in.

SHINTO Japanese animistic religion, meaning way of the gods. It is based on ancestor worship.

SHORINJI KEMPO Japanese karate system founded by Doshin So, its first headmaster. Following his death the organization is now headed by his daughter.

SHOTOKAN School of Japanese karate founded by Gichin Funakoshi. Name derives from Funakoshi's pen name, shoto. Probably the most widely practiced style of karate in the world.

SHURIKEN Throwing stars, originally made of iron and sharply pointed. The favorite weapon of the ninja. Many different shapes and sizes existed.

SHUAI CHIAO One of the earliest organized fighting systems in China, dating back to around 700 BC. A form of wrestling, but with few throws. Today it is an official sport of the People's Repubic of China.

SIFU An instructor in kung fu (the word means father) who is identified with the Japanese sensei.

SIL LUM Cantonese name for the Shaolin Temple.

SIL LIM TAO The first form in wing chun (the word means little idea or little imagination). This form teaches elbow positioning and protection of the centerline. There are no foot movements involved.

SO JUTSU The Japanese skill of using the spear (the word means art of the spear).

SPARRING Combat. It gives a karate student the means to apply the various techniques he or she has learned.

SPORT KARATE Karate competition in which contestants wear protective gloves and foot pads.

SWEEP A technique which catches the opponent's feet to unbalance him.

SUMO Ancient form of Japanese wrestling steeped in quasi-religious aspects of Shintoism. Contestants build themselves up to great weights on very rich diets to gain the advantage over an opponent.

SUN TZU or TSU The author of the Chinese military classic *The Art of War*. Believed by many to be the treatise upon which ninjutsu is based. This classic is still read today in military academies the world over.

TAEKWONDO Korean style of empty-hand combat, very similar to Japanese karate, in which great emphasis is placed upon delivering strikes with the feet and fists. This art was partly indigenous to Korea, being known as tae kyon, an older version and the forerunner of today's style.

TAI CHI CHUAN Tai chi, as it is now more commonly known, is one of the three internal systems of kung fu. Greatly valued for its therapeutic powers in relieving stress and tension and creating a state of peace and tranquility. The movements form a continuous flowing action, as each technique merges into the next. The art is performed at a very slow speed.

There is also a deadly side to tai chi, but it is only known by a few instructors. The name means grand or great ultimate fist.

TAMASIWARA Japanese technique of striking the body against materials such as wood, tiles, bricks, ice and so on, to test the power or force of a strike. In recent times new records have been set by various martial artists, demolishing even larger piles of solid objects.

TANG SOO DO Means way of the tang hand. This Korean martial art is very similar to Japanese shotokan karate. The style was developed by Hang Kee in 1949, based upon, he claims, t'ang su and suak, both ancient forms of Korean martial arts.

TAO Chinese term meaning path or way. Tao is an invisible force or energy, present in all things in the universe.

TE Okinawan term meaning hand.

THAI BOXING *see* **MUAY THAI.**

THAING A general term for the Burmese art of self-defense.

TOBOK Suit or tunic worn by practitioners of taekwondo, consisting of a loose shirt and pants tied in the middle with a sash or belt.

TONFA Okinawan agricultural weapon (once the handle used to operate a manual millstone) adopted by the native Okinawans to fight the invading Japanese when weapons were banned. Used in karate to improve technique. In recent times many American police departments have developed their own tonfa to replace the standard billy club or night stick.

TIGER One of the five animals in Shaolin kung fu.

URUMI An Indian spring-sword with four very sharp edges.

UESHIBA Morihei Ueshiba, the founder of aikido.

VITAL POINTS Certain areas of the body which, when struck in a particular way by a great master, cause great pain and even death.

WADO RYU KARATE A style of Japanese karate developed from shotokan by Hironori Ohtsuka. The name means way of peace school.

WHITE BELT In most Japanese martial arts, the white belt indicates a beginner.

WAZARI A score of half a point in competition martial arts. It is awarded for skillful technique. One full point is termed an ippon which is usually given when a contestant executes a flawless technique.

WING CHUN Chinese martial art, invented by a woman named Yim Wing Chun, is considered one of the most effective forms of kung fu. The governing principle is economy of motion. Wing Chun greatly influenced Bruce Lee when he was formulating his own eclectic system of jeet kune do. Wing Chun means beautiful springtime.

WU SHU A Chinese term meaning military arts. Now used as a generic name for the highly acrobatic martial arts of mainland China.

YANG The positive aspect of the universe in Chinese cosmology. Yang signifies male and light, one half of the Taoist view of the universe which is characterized by positive action.

YANG STYLE Yang style tai chi was developed by Yang Lu Chan in the early part of the nineteenth century. The yang method contains the original 13 postures of tai chi.

YARI A Japanese straight-bladed spear about eight feet long which replaced the naginata as a battlefield weapon. So far as is known the yari never developed into the sporting form of 'do.'

YIN The negative aspect of the universe in Chinese cosmology. Relates to emptiness, softness and darkness, and the female principle. Yin is symbolized by the black fish with the white eye in the famous yin-yang symbol.

YOKO ARUKI One of the secret walking techniques of the ninja. By employing such methods, the ninja did not reveal in which direction he was travelling, so making it difficult for his enemies to track him. The term means walking sideways.

YOKOZUNA The grand champion rank of sumo wrestling. This is the highest of the five ranks.

YUDANSHA A kendoka who has achieved the rank of black belt or higher. Only those of yudansha rank are permitted to wear an outfit that has a uniform color.

ZANSHIN A state of mind cultivated in many Japanese martial arts. The practitioner is calm and aware of his opponent's every movement.

ZEN Religious philosophy that claims that one can reach satori, or enlightenment, through meditation. Founded by the Indian monk and holy man Bodhidharma. Zen makes use of illogical poems called koans to clear the mind of trivia and so reach a meditative state of mind. In China, Zen is called chan or ch'an. Zen was much favored by the Japanese samurai.

ZHURKANE A Persian or Iranian term meaning powerhouse. A system of highly specialized strength exercises; apparently this martial art is 3000 years old, dating back to the court of Darius. Zhurkane was supposed to be the martial art system ued for training Darius's personal bodyguard.

Index

The author wishes to thank
the following people for
their invaluable assistance:
Pat Cronshaw of *Oriental
World*, Manchester,
England; Mr Danny
Connor; Mr Bruce Ayling of
Fighters magazine; Terry
O'Neill of *Fighting Arts*
magazine; and Mr David
Moore. the publisher would
like to thank Mandy Little
the picture researcher,
Adrian Hodgkins the
designer, Ron Watson for
preparing the index and the
individuals and agencies
listed below for supplying
the photographs.

All-Sport: page 92 (top right), 130
    (bottom), 131, 152, 153 (both),
    164, 165
Anglo-Chinese Educational Inst:
    page 35, 12
BBC Hulton Picture Library: page
    6-7, 10 (bottom), 105 (both), 106
    (top) 177, 185 (top)
Camera Press Ltd: page 123 (both)
Paul Coleman: page 82 (top), 88 (top
    three)
Silvio Dockov: page 71 (top right &
    left), 89 (top two), 93 (both), 95
    (bottom), 99, 159, 160 (top), 161
Condor Books: page 143
Condor Books/Robert A. Bussey:
    page 2-3, 141
Condor Books/Geri Gilbert: page
    138, 139 (bottom)
Condor Books/Kirtland C Peterson:
    page 145
CFW Enterprises, Inc. (Inside Kung
    Fu): page 1, 4-5, 8-9, 18-19, 22, 23
    (centre and bottom left), 36-37,
    38, 43, 52, 61 (bottom), 64 (right),

65, 92 (top left), 97, 116 (top), 134-
    35, 137, 140, 142 (top), 163, 167,
    170-71, 172, 184-85, 188
Douglas Dickins Photo Library:
    page 102-03, 176 (top right)
Archiv Gerstenberg: page 106
    (bottom right), 107, 116 (bottom)
Jane Hallander: page 20 (top &
    bottom), 21, 41, 44, 62 (top &
    bottom), 63, 79 (bottom), 111
    (both), 114 (top), 148, 150-51, 156,
    157, 168 (all three), 169
Norma Harvey: page 69, 72 (top), 77
    (top), 78 (left), 79 (top), 83 (right),
    86, 87 (both), 90 (bottom), 95
    (top), 101 (bottom), 120-21, 128,
    154, 163 (bottom left), 179, 184
    (left), 186
The Hutchinson Library: page 14-
    15, 15 (bottom), 17, 110-111, 115,
    118
Japanese Tourist Board: page 94-95,
    108-09, 112
Field Museum of Natural History,
    Chicago: page 10 (top), 14
Joel Finlar: page 54 (left all four)
Peter Lewis: page 24 (top &
    bottom), 25, 26, 27, 28 (both), 29
    (both), 30 (all four), 31 (both), 32-
    33, 39, 40 (both), 45 (all three), 46
    (both), 47 (both), 48, 49, 50 (all
    three), 51, 61 (top), 64 (left), 68, 71
    (bottom), 75 (both), 76, 77
    (bottom), 78 (top right), 80, 81, 82
    (bottom), 83 (left), 84 (all eight),
    90 (top), 92 (bottom two), 98
    (both), 100 (both), 101 (top), 104,
    114 (bottom two), 125 (top), 127
    (all three), 136, 137 (bottom left),
    139 (top), 142 (bottom), 143
    (bottom), 144 (bottom), 146 (all
    three), 147 (all three), 149 (both),
    155, 173 (all six), 176 (top right &
    bottom), 178, 180, 181 (both), 187,
    189 (bottom)
James Maton: page 66-67, 70, 74, 88
    (bottom two), 89 (bottom two),
    85, 96
National Film Archive, London:
    page 53, 54 (top right), 55 (both),
    57, 58, 59, 189 (top)
Peter Newark's Historical Pictures:
    page 34 (top), 106 (bottom left),
    113 (top)
James Rousseau: page 72 (top), 182
Bob Thomas Sports Photography:
    page 130 (top two), 160 (bottom)
TPS/Keystone: page 94 (top), 113
    (bottom), 124 (bottom), 125
    (bottom), 126, 174, 175 (both)
TPS/Three Lions: page 108, 109, 124
    (top), 128-129, 129, 133 (bottom)
Victoria & Albert Museum,
    London: page 122
Xinhua News Agency: page 11, 34-
    35, 35 (bottom right), 37 (both)